JOHN CAIRNEY made his stage debut at the Park Theatre, Glasgow, before enrolling at the RSAMD in Glasgow. After graduation, he joined the Wilson Barrett Company as Snake in *The School for Scandal*. A season at the Glasgow Citizens Theatre followed before going on to the Bristol Old Vic where he appeared in the British premiere of Arthur Miller's *The Crucible*. He returned to the Citizens from time to time, most notably as Hamlet in 1960. He also appeared in the premiere of John Arden's *Armstrong's Last Goodnight* in 1964. Other stage work until 1991 included King Humanitie in *The Thrie Estaites* for Tyrone Guthrie at the Edinburgh Festival, Archie Rice in *The Entertainer* at Dundee (1972), Cyrano de Bergerac at Newcastle (1974), Becket in *Murder in the Cathedral* at the Edinburgh Festival of 1986 and Macbeth in the same Festival in 1989. He also wrote and appeared in his own productions of *An Edinburgh Salon, At Your Service, The Ivor Novello Story* and *A Mackintosh Experience* while continuing to tour the world in his solo *The Robert Burns Story*.

His association with Burns began in 1965 with Tom Wright's solo play *There Was a Man* at the Traverse Theatre, Edinburgh, and at the Arts Theatre, London. The solo was televised twice nationally and was also an album recording for REL Records, Edinburgh, as well as a video for Green Place Productions, Glasgow. From Burns he moved on to other solos on William McGonagall, Robert Service and Robert Louis Stevenson until he worked with New Zealand actress, Alannah O'Sullivan at the Edinburgh Festival of 1978. They married in 1980. As 'Two for a Theatre' they toured the world for P&O Cruises and the British Council as well as the Keedick Lecture Bureau, New York, with programmes on Byron, Wilde and Dorothy Parker until 1986.

Cairney's first film was *Ill Met by Moonlight* for the Rank Organisation, followed by *Windom's Way, Victim, Shake Hands with the Devil* and many more including *Jason and the Argonauts* and *Cleopatra, Devil Ship Pirates* and *Study in Terror* in 1965. His many television parts include Branwell Brontë, Edgar Allan Poe and Robert Bruce and he has featured in all the main series: *Danger Man, The Avengers, Dr Finlay's Casebook, Elizabeth R, Jackanory* and *Taggart*. He also starred in BBC2's *This Man Craig*, which ran for two years, 1966–68. In addition, he wrote and recorded his own songs for EMI at Abbey Road.

As a writer, Cairney has published two autobiographies, two novels and three books on Scottish football. He has written eight books for Luath Press, including three on the life and works of Burns, biographies of Robert Louis Stephenson and Charles Rennie Mackintosh, a book of essays on Glasgow entitled *Glasgow, by the way, but*, and a book on acting called Greasepaint Monkey. His next book, *The Tycoon and the Bard*, about Andrew Carnegie and Robert Burns, is now in progress.

In his free time, Cairney watches football, paints, listens to classical music, reads non-fiction and enjoys occasional moments of silence.

Cairney gained an M.Litt from Glasgow University for A History of Solo Theatre in 1988 and, in 1994, a PhD from Victoria University, Wellington, for his study, Stevenson and Theatre. Having spent the last 17 years in New Zealand, John and Alannah returned to live again in Glasgow in 2008.

The Importance of
BEING

Observations from my Anecdotage

JOHN CAIRNEY

Luath Press Limited
EDINBURGH
www.luath.co.uk

First published 2014

ISBN: 978-1-910021-08-8

The publishers acknowledge the support of

ALBA | CHRUTHACHAIL

towards the publication of this volume.

The paper used in this book is recyclable. It is made from
low chlorine pulps produced in a low energy, low emissions manner
from renewable forests.

Printed and bound by
Bell & Bain Ltd., Glasgow

Typeset in 11 point Sabon
by 3btype.com

To the unknown lady
in Edinburgh Central Library,
who first gave me the idea for and title of this book.

By the same author

Contents

The Four Quarters of Life

In the first quarter, we are made,
In the second quarter, we make our way,
In the third quarter, we make our mark,
In the fourth quarter, we make our peace.

Preface

The meaning of life is that it stops.
FRANZ KAFKA

WHAT IS IT TO be a human being? Is it only to be human? Or is it just *being*? Socrates said, 'To do, is to be.' What is *to be*? And what can we *do*? The answer is that we keep breathing. This may seem obvious but it is surprising how often this basic process is disregarded. It serves here as a starting point, the aboriginal fact in a consideration of being as far as it is reflected in this writer's life and work and overall existence. To exist at all is only a matter of ventilation, a need to comply with the need to breathe in and out. A simple act, it reminds us that being alive comes down to the plain fact of being awake. If the heart is beating, a person is there. This primitive action is often overlooked or taken for granted in the hurrying, striving, contemporary days that are the early decades of the 21st century. We are all subject to mortality, which means, frankly, that we are dying from the moment we are born.

Why is it then, that we patently ignore the fact that all we really know at any given moment is the *now* we are in. We can remember the moment gone, whether a minute since or years ago, and we can reasonably assume the near future, but we don't really *know* what is yet to happen.

Which is why, whatever or wherever our lives as we live them, the present is there to be relished; to be enjoyed for the very joy it holds or whatever satisfaction can be extracted from it, no matter how dismal the current scenario may seem. Nothing lasts forever, certainly not life itself. In these supposedly civilised and sophisticated times, no one appears to accept the moment for the present it is and revel in the free gift that is the day at hand. The focus always seems to be on the vague possibility of things, the reward that lies just over the horizon. In my view, the real answer is always right at hand, it is in us, and immediately about us, awaiting our notice. Is it only missed because it's so obvious?

Wiser minds than mine have tried to tell us this truth down the centuries, but they were ignored or dismissed as irrelevant or eccentric, simply because the concentric mass, whatever the era, is always too preoccupied in surviving materially in a competitive world.

These thoughts have only occurred to me now because I am now old, and a survivor. Survival may be all but it isn't everything. No one was more competitive than I when young, but over a long lifetime, my all-consuming, selfish ambitions have been gradually crushed out of my mind by the dead weight they are. I can literally be called light-headed today, because I've shed a lot of rubbish from the vanity bag I carried throughout a long, hectic career as a professional actor. I've finally broken out of my own, self-imposed bubble. I'm free now to concentrate on living's only priority – catching the moment when I can, enjoying the passing hour and making the most of every day. Basically, I'm just glad to be.

This is not to be smug. Far from it. My knees are not what they were, the arms are drained of muscle mass, the hearing is suspect and the heart has a stent in it, but that same heart is pounding with enthusiasm for life, real life, not its hybrid imitation, which is accepted by most from what they see and hear around them. My own mind is continually racing with ideas. Why couldn't I have felt this spilling-over of vivacity years ago? But that's only one of life's lessons – we learn as we go. Yet why are we so punished for growing old? Why should we lose much of our faculties, just when we're really beginning to know how to use them? This is an irony that continues to be one of life's puzzles.

Looking back over life, at least as I have known it, I see that it is a time of cries, a series of appeals at every stage, heard as the baby leaves the womb for the crib, then goes from the crib to the nursery pen, from there finding the freedom to stumble to the front door and, on firmer legs, takes the first steps out into the world. In life's second quarter, the adolescent seeks the freedom to explore. It is a time of flux. The cry here is for attention so that what we are doing can be seen and applauded, and if not, put away to try any alternative that will meet the continuing changes. The cry of the third quarter is for acknowledgement, for justification, proof that you have done well. If not, there's still time to make it right if you have the will. In the last quarter there is only one cry and that is for mercy, for forgiveness, but we have cried out so much in life that we are hoarse and can only whisper, 'I'm sorry!'

Choices arise regularly and have to be met. For instance, you have chosen to read this book. Which means you have given time to it. Let's face it, a book is a luxury of the reading classes. Today there are so many alternative means of passing time, being entertained, or imparting or receiving information available to the public, that to buy or borrow a book to read, for any reason, is to make a superior statement of intent. Once any book is taken up, a definite aim to read it is assumed. Should you do so, you obviously don't have toothache, or a bad tummy, and have no desperate worries. More importantly, you have the time to surrender to another's printed opinions and/or imaginings.

Every book is a private conversation between reader and author, unless the book is being read to someone, then it is a performance, and the reader an actor. For the most part, however, it is a complicit act between two consenting parties. The following pages are a conversation with myself, which I cordially invite the reader to overhear as a very welcome third party. The main narrative takes me from infancy to near senility, giving me an opportunity to unburden the weight of things done; of seeing the experiences of a crowded lifetime for what they are: merely incidents and happenings along the way.

The essential person that we are continues throughout, affected for better or worse by the very act of living. This is what will be examined as each stage is explored. I shall try to scrape away the self and reveal the Id, which prefaces the entity we are and creates what we know as 'identity', which is what we are seen to be. I may then be able to look at myself honestly and see my 'self' – what I really am, just another example of a striving man.

Any one life describes the progress of an age as it has changed down the centuries. That being said, mankind *per se* remains the same. Only our material environment is altered. I don't know the baby I was, I've almost forgotten the boy I must have been or the young man I became and the older man I am now is completely foreign to me, a total mystery. These phases are the signposts on which we hang the faces we present, the masks we hide behind as we grow. These selves are almost strangers to each other, even to ourselves, but they are, in their sum, what we really are.

I have laid out the line of my own life so that I can hang out the washing of my personal observations and arrive at some kind of conclusion about why we are all here in the first place. What use did I make of the life given me at birth? After all, it was a gift, a present, not to keep, but to be used, on loan, for a certain term. The rent due is the return one makes on the investment, and is counted in terms of every day lived. This calls for concentrated effort, integrity and objectivity, traits I have worked on over the years and, hopefully, I may have reached the stage, at last, where I can trust myself to say what I mean.

We still have the voices we were born with. It is something that is in us and is unique to us. This is everyone's mark, our stamp, and we want it known. Basically, it's the same impulse that compels people to daub their names on walls, carve their initials on trees or scrawl graffiti in inaccessible places. They only want to tell the world, 'Look! I am here! I am alive! I exist! I have being!' Whatever we do or say, we can never make a bigger statement than that. Life is there for the taking. We can elect to take it or leave it to float by as it will. If we have the confidence we can reach out and grab it as it passes. Or, if we are lucky, it will reach out and open up to us. The path will suddenly appear and each of us will then be faced with a decision: do we take it and find out who we really are by doing what we want to do, or do we meekly accept what it throws at us along the way and conform? Decisions are there to be made at every turn, that's what life's about. On the choices we make, depend the lives we lead.

In my time, I have survived an earthquake, a hurricane at sea and being shot at (twice). I have been inside a pyramid, walked over Red Square, sailed up the Yangtze River and down the Suez Canal, and I have seen much of what is between both Poles. I have been applauded, derided, switched on and switched off, loved much and actively disliked – but I have never hated, *really* hated, anyone or anything. I'm glad to say that. I know now that I only fully exist when in complete relation to everything else that lives and breathes around me. I believe that everyone's life is a story, that my story is yours, and your story mine. That is the tale I want to tell.

As a working actor, published author, selling artist and sometime academic, I have a harvestable field to work from; at the very least, I can claim a right to put forward a point of view. Call it an attempt to unearth and illustrate, by anecdote and/or comment, those interior areas in our lives that are common to us all.

What I have written might be described as a hymn to growing old. I like to think that this volume is my *Book of Hours*. That I wrote it by candlelight, with a good fountain pen, into the lined pages of an old ledger, sitting at a wide desk under the window while 'Vespers' were being sung in the distance. Instead, it is my *Book of Years*, stabbed out with two fingers on a temperamental computer, while wearing a tracksuit and listening to BBC Radio 3. My publisher has wrapped around these pages a cover that features the dashboard of a car and a rear-view mirror with my own eyes looking out. In these pages, I'm looking back on the long road I have come, seeing my existence through all its parts. Any life is one long paper chase, from the birth certificate to the death notice, with papers of all kinds in between: school reports, medical reports, exam results, graduation certificates, love letters, wedding certificates, divorce certificates, press notices, parking fines, citations, correspondence, and finally, the obituary.

By which time, we will know more than anyone about life and ourselves. We may perhaps wonder why we bothered so much about the unimportant tomorrow or left it so late to understand the precious *now*. It all comes down to nothing more than being heard or seen. What else prompts a person to put down on paper their closest thoughts, secret hopes or wildest speculations? After all, a writer's voice has to be seen before it is heard.

Introduction

ROBERT BURNS, in the Introduction to his Second Commonplace book in 1787, wrote:

> I don't know how it is with the world in general, but with me, making my remarks is by no means a solitary pleasure – I want some one to laugh with me, to be grave with me, some one to please me and help my discrimination with his or her own remark, and at times, no doubt, to admire my acuteness and penetration.
>
> The world are so busied with selfish pursuits, ambition, vanity, interest, or pleasure, that very few think it worth their while to make any observation on what passes around them, except where that observation is a sucker or branch of the darling plant they are rearing in their fancy. Nor am I sure, notwithstanding all the sentimental flights of Novel writers, and the sage philosophy of Moralists, whether we are capable of so intimate and cordial a coalition of friendship as that one man can pour out his bosom, his every thought and floating fancy, his very inmost soul, with unreserved confidence to another without hazard of losing part of that respect which man deserves from man –
>
> For these reasons, I am determined to make these pages my Confidante. I will sketch every character... to the best of my power, I will insert anecdotes and take down remarks ... where I hit on anything clever, my own applause will, in some measure, feast my vanity.
>
> My own private story likewise, my love-adventures, my rambles, the frowns and smiles of Fortune on my Bardship, my Poems and fragments that must never see the light shall be occasionally inserted. In short, never did a [book price] purchase so much friendship, since Confidence went first to market, or Honesty was set up to sale.

LIFE FOR ALL OF US is no more than an accumulation of days, a succession of sleeps. Our finite state, our common mortality, gives us a sense of belonging to the tribe, of *being*. And that's what makes it important. That's what determined the title of this book. The finished volume has been slow in developing, but the original idea for the project came from the four lines shown on page nine that first came into my head while driving around the earthquake city of Christchurch, New Zealand, during February 2011. Time passed, but the words stayed in my head until November 2012, when, in Edinburgh, I was due to give a reading of my solo presentation on Robert Louis Stevenson in the Central Library. After the performance, I was at a table signing copies of my Stevenson book when a well-dressed, well-spoken lady approached for an autograph.

'I do hope you write that book?' she said.

'What book?' I asked as I scribbled my signature.

'*The Importance of Being*,' she replied. 'Lovely title. I'd buy it.'

That was the spark that set the whole idea going. One chance remark, casually made, was enough to tie it to the few lines from Christchurch and I knew I had the frame of something. The importance of being. But the importance of being what? Like everyone else, 'Earnest' was the first thing that came to mind. As much as I admire Oscar's word skills, I am just as earnest in putting forward 'being' as an orphan among words. It is rarely used in its proper context, which is as the basic description of the human condition. It is usually a twin, holding hands with other words, so that we get 'being sad', 'being happy', etc, but I am being particular in this case, defining 'being' first and foremost, as the term used to describe our elementary physical existence as members of the human race.

Then I remembered why the lady had picked up the phrase. I had ad-libbed on this 'being' theme before starting on my script only because I was so pleased to see a full house.

'I'm delighted to be here tonight,' I began, then broke off to say, 'In fact, at my age, I'm delighted to be anywhere!'

This got an immediate, warm response and encouraged me to continue playing on the 'to be' idea and to link it with the Kiwi lines. All this came out quite spontaneously and may only have lasted five minutes, but it did include a snippet from Hamlet's 'To be, or not to be? That is the question...' To me, there was no question, but I then remembered I had a show to do. I got on with the RLS performance and, ironically, the first line of the script was uncannily apposite –

'We all invent ourselves in our own lives but we don't always get the opportunity to play as cast.'

This only added fuel to the idea, but the whole concept burst into flame for me after I saw a film at the Glasgow Film Theatre early in 2013. It was called *I Am Breathing* and was made by two young filmmakers, Emma Davie and Morag McKinnon. It concerned a 37-year-old architect, Neil Platt, a Scot working in London, happily married and with a baby girl. Neil was suddenly struck down in his 30s by Motor Neurone Disease. His slow dissolution was movingly filmed in his home and by the end of the film everyone in the cinema that day was in tears. The stress of the narrative was in the importance shown to the simple act of breathing in and out, which was the only difference to Neil Platt's being alive or dead. This was exactly the theme I had been looking for, and, from that moment, I not only wanted to write this book, I knew I had to.

Are any of us really the person we want to be? Or are we only what life so far has made us out of the bumps, scrapes, mountain peaks, valleys and troughs of everyday existence? Is it that simple? What is it we're all looking for? Is it all a big mirage? Are we only the heart-hinge between what has been and what will be? As Robert Burns points out, the heart has it:

Nae treasures nor pleasures could make us happy lang,
The heart's ay the part ay that maks us richt or wrang,
Catch the moments as they fly, use them as ye ought, man.
Believe me, happiness is shy and comes not ay when sought, man...

It is always difficult to catch these flying moments because we are either fretting about what has passed or worrying about what is to come. We are reassured by the past because we know that it did happen, that we survived, and it can be remembered, but the future is an uncertain quantity and we are all, subconsciously, afraid of the unknown. Being, however, is not memory, nor is it speculation. It is here and now, and with us continually. Contentment in the present, therefore, should be our priority. We have to bear in mind that, as long as we are warm, fed, clothed and, best of all, loved, we have no reason to complain of our state of being. It is always at hand and at our service. It is meant to be enjoyed or at least provide proof of our 'being' at any given time.

Meantime, we survive in the consciousness of the four constant states available to us, the physical, mental, emotional and spiritual props that uphold our very fabric. As long as we engage in life at all of its stages, fully and fearlessly, then we're living and that is reason enough to be grateful. As I said, ventilation is the key, a continuing wind function, breath coming and going, burping and farting, air relentlessly refreshing and renewing all our body parts. That's living.

Mankind, however, is more than a physical phenomenon. He is a thinking animal with a body apparatus that is a miracle of physical and intellectual efficiency, which is sadly underused in today's increasingly spectator world. If we really used all that was within us to its full force, we could touch the very heart of things. We could be our own worldwide web, but in our over-informed, sophisticated age, the focus is always on exterior show and tomorrow's great plan. Of course, we must sensibly plan ahead, but we must never lose sight of where we are at the time, or forget that the present is the place where the real living is done. How right to say, 'How good this is!' when it is. It frames the moment and sets it up in our minds.

We can't exist properly on the possibility of things. The real answers are always available because they are in us and about us. Solutions are always at hand. Our first concern should be to concentrate on the essentials, taking time to listen, talking less and enjoying the silence. It provides that special moment, wherever and however it happens. Silence is a good place but good silence is a rarity. It is not golden, as the saying has it, it is platinum. It should be welcomed like a much-loved visitor. Above all, be slow to break it. Just be glad to *be*.

'To be' in Latin is *esse*. Thus we get the word's essence, and the essence of existence is the compulsion to keep on living. It also gives us the word 'essential', which appears to be the most misused word of the century, since it applies to things that are really quite unessential to living, like the internet, social media, electronic toys, fast cars and fast food, every kind of gadget, money lending and almost any kind of insurance. Values and standards change almost on the hour. It's no wonder people are bewildered by the lack of tried and familiar certainties. It is time to rediscover the old-fashioned sureties like family connections, personal relationships, writing real letters by hand, talking with friends face to face, finding time for contemplation, economy of diet, and a wardrobe bought for utility, not show.

By all means let us enjoy our hobbies, but know they are only for leisure. On the other hand, we must pursue our projects relentlessly. These need time and application and often a little luck, but what is luck, after all, but Providence with a blindfold? It is the underground swell that carries along the surface tide and we have sometimes to lie back and trust that occasionally our needs and opportunity coincide. This is serendipity. Except that we are often the last to notice. The first essential for the good life is optimism, but the most valuable, by far, is the faculty it spawns: enthusiasm. This might be our most important attribute, for it is well nigh impossible to do anything worthwhile without it.

Once embarked on any enterprise, the next asset is sheer persistence; never to lose heart, whatever the setbacks. Persistence is a virtue sadly underestimated, for it is associated principally with diligence, a dull slogging away, yet without it, many greater projects than just another book would never see the light. No matter the seeming impossibility of overcoming the problem or removing the obstacle, we soon find that Robert W. Service was right in his view that everything either blows hot or cold or away.

Tomorrow's worry is today's nuisance and both are only a souvenir of a long-gone yesterday. 'If only' is a phrase that we should drop from our vocabulary. It is emotional sabotage. The 'if' is conditional on so many things, and 'only' limits the choice to one. So, we made the wrong decision. It wasn't fatal, was it? So forget it and get on with the next wrong decision. We can too easily make an enemy of our own selves. It may be, subconsciously, that we are afraid of ourselves. We are all, in a sense, entirely of our own making.

We don't see ourselves in others as we should. We are all one of many, yet, paradoxically, each of us is unique. Each of us is original but we are not apart. Nobody in the world is anonymous. We all fit in the one great design. We only have to recognise our place in the jigsaw. Find your target and run towards it, take a flying leap. Taking the leap, that's what living is about. As the old Zen saying has it: 'Leap and the net will appear.'

All I know for certain is that that I'm not certain of anything. In the writing of this manuscript, other people everywhere have been my true guides and mentors, and I shall remain grateful to all of them, many of them ordinary people like ourselves. Although, that's my first lie. There are no ordinary people. We are all, in our various ways, quite extraordinary and that is principally what I want to celebrate here. *I'm only human, after all* should not be an apology or an excuse, but a celebration.

This book, if you like, is a book of wisdom – folk wisdom, 'folk' meaning the people I've met. They are the canvas on which the narrative is painted, and the result owes more to observation and memory than to any hard study. It may be no worse for that. I want to explore the life theme imaginatively and take the opportunity wherever possible to extend the thought, improvise on it if need be. The matter owes much to things read, overheard, talked about, thought about or wondered at, even picked up casually. Especially when it is fun. For instance, in our hairdresser's recently, a well-dressed, fussy woman was complaining that she had been sitting unattended for at least five minutes: 'I've got to be in Comrie in an hour,' she complained. Tommy, the hairdresser, was unfazed, and in his typical Glasgow way replied, 'Have no fear, Ma'm, Comrie's been there for a thousand years, and it's likely to still be there in an hour.'

Or again: one summer afternoon, I was carrying home a large painting canvas, all wrapped up and just bought from the art shop. A passing Glaswegian in overalls said, without breaking his stride on the pavement, 'Geez, that's some pizza!'

Even the passers-by laughed.

Then, on the bus recently, an older couple came on, arguing quietly in the way of long married couples. I stood up to let them have my double seat and moved to sit in the single opposite. This, however, was quickly occupied by the woman.

'I'm sorry,' I said, 'I thought you were married.'

'We ur,' said the wife. 'That's how we never sit thegither.'

I shrugged and said nothing, but sat down dutifully beside the husband, who whispered to me, 'It gies us baith a bit o' peace.'

But I noticed the twinkle in his eye.

Lastly. It was in a Glasgow street, outside Sainsbury's, not so long ago. As I emerged with a full plastic bag in each hand, a woman stopped me at the door, and asked me quite seriously: 'Excuse me, did you used to be John Cairney?'

We are Made

In the first quarter
We are made,
Displayed,
All parts intact,
All systems go,
Except you don't know
What to do with yourself.
Your mouth pressed on a small, soft hill
And held until
A smooth, warm liquid
Fills your entire being.
It stills your fears,
Stops your tears.
Why weep?
When all you want to do is sleep.
You are only one of millions born
At that moment, torn
From the comforting womb
And hurled into a room
Of cold wind, noise and light
That hurts your eyes, closed tight
Not daring
To see this place, not caring
To hear their cheers
As all alone
A helpless handful of flesh and bone
Is thrust with force into time and place
As part of what they call the human race.

CHAPTER ONE

Infancy

If you must create something, you must be something.

GOETHE

JAMES LOVELOCK'S 1970s Gaia theory, named for the Greek goddess who symbolised Mother Earth, suggests that everything created was in creation from the beginning, it just took time to emerge from its microscopic origins to become the vast, multi-universe we now know. We can then accept that the tiniest events in nature can have enormous repercussions, which can, in some cases, lead to chaos. The smallest actions can lead to the biggest happenings and there is no smaller action than the development of the seed in the womb, nor a bigger repercussion than the resulting birth of another human being. We still have in us all the apparatus for living we were given at the first moment of life. The difference is that it is now con-ditioned, not only by environment and education, but by what has been absorbed subconsciously as we develop. We have been dealt our life-cards and it's up to us to learn how to play them in this wonderful, exciting and unpredictable gamble called existence.

It is our only decided certainty, the sole definition accepted, that to be alive is to have being, to live now – right now – and with the means to grow into our full potential. We are a continuing part of the primordial process begun when someone or something crawled out of the sea or fell from a tree. Whether we were originally aquatic or arboreal is irrelevant. We have begun, therefore the only requirement is to keep going. For just as the universe started with the action of the smallest atom in space, the hardly perceptible first movement in the womb is our practical start, the miniscule event from which comes our history, all the epic deeds of mortal man and the highest heights of human thought or artistic creation.

What is plain to see in our story as a species is that humankind's greatest skill is not only in creating human life, but in replicating itself, making itself anew from generation unto generation with unstoppable energy, thus firmly establishing the unvarying process of procreation. The copyright for the original process may lie elsewhere, but it is humanity's primal act. Like the earth's action, it is a never-ending cycle, based on similar collisions or junctions involving physical matter at every stage. Bumps certainly do occur and this can be seen readily in the gradual expansion of the female outline over the required nine months of pregnancy.

I never cease to be amazed at how our spinning globe, a pre-ordained conglomeration of minerals, metals and molecules, over countless centuries can make mountains. And still does. Even to my uninformed ear, stories of our human and our world's beginnings still fascinate, no matter who or what the real originator might be. The narrative itself is still a matter of wonder. So many tiny factors conspiring to create objects of mammoth proportions. It is a universal phenomenon. Applied to the generation of life itself, mammoth proportions are not looked for and the tiny things involved are babies.

This latest specimen of human life has been arrived at by an incredible harmony of disparate events. Events that still occur today. But so does an inherent harmony, whatever the climate change, and where there is harmony, some-body must be calling the tune. But who, or what? We may never know. Meantime, perhaps the most important of all world events is birth. Human birth. It is a purely animal exercise, no different for a fox in the forest or a polar bear on an ice cap. A little version of a bigger one forces its way out on a given day in a given way and the species continues, whether through the birth pangs of a cosseted royal under the media blanket, or of a single mother under an overcoat in a rented back room.

A birth of any kind has all the importance of the remote black hole to us earthbound creatures, except that we know exactly how it began and what is the likely outcome. As with the principal of natural selection, the phenomenon of human birth goes through all its preliminary stages before the necessary explosion that announces its happening. It is, in fact, a miniscule replaying of that super-celestial action taking place even now above our heads. It is indeed above our heads and completely beyond our understanding, if we will only admit it. There might be no end to the universe. So why don't we just get on with what we've got while we have it?

We are an assorted mixture of bits and pieces all functioning in concert while healthy but given to painful discordance when any part of the whole fails to function. Human *being* is not just an adjectival noun, it's a living fact. At least we all know where it starts. It begins, in most cases at least, because of that greatest of all imperatives in life – LOVE. Even the word itself is a pleasure to say, compared to how one spits out its alternative, 'hate'. Which one says with a quick breath and a hard 't', but we have to wait with the word 'love', lingering on the labial first letter, which loiters in the mouth as if reluctant to come out. It then flows on to the lips to make the fricative 'v'-sound that ends the lovely word. This is perhaps why it is one of the most used of words and probably, at the same time, the most abused. It can indicate a liking for chocolate biscuits or an undying affection for another human and every emotion in between.

Love is all-embracing and is a two-way phenomenon. If you give your heart to someone, that someone must give a heart back in exchange, if the process is to work. It is the only thing we give and take freely and wholly without question. Best of all, it is spontaneous. If there is any calculation or planning in it, then it's not love, but lust or material ambition. Real love has its own energy and is carried forward in a wave that is irresistible. Sentimental, or superficial love, arises from affection, and is merely the spray that rises from the real thing. Deep love, freely given, is rarely refused. The successful formula is where love begets love and the sharers, the giver and the recipient, store it up between themselves so that the supply never dries up and can be used again and again over a lifetime, like a millwheel turning with the steady supply of water from the running stream. Or, it is the flower that mustn't be allowed to wilt. If cared for and tended, it's for life. It is only when love is static and inorganic that its impact diminishes and fades. If hoarded selfishly, or misused, or taken for granted, it rots and dies, and there is nothing sadder than a dead love or an ex-lover. But there is nothing more heart-lifting than two people who are in love and living it.

Love is part of our survival chemistry. No one should be denied it. It is a right due to us as a collective. We were meant to live alongside each other for safety, for survival, for reassurance, for comfort. First as a family, then as a tribe in a village, neighbours in a town, acquaintances in a city and so it goes on and up and outward until it spreads our connection all round the world like a huge net of every kind of multi-coloured material. It is this net, however, that keeps us connected and together as a species. Despite our constant squabbles over superficial differences, we are still intended to live as one family. Man and woman as a species are identical except in that specific physical area where their sexual apparatus varies. One protrudes where the other recedes, but men have the beginning of breasts on their hairy chests. A split-second action in the womb is what makes them male or female, but to all other intents they are exactly similar with neither being inferior or superior to the other. They may dress differently, but that is mere social habit and not fundamental to their persona. There may also be a genuine, same-sex attraction which has a contemporary acceptance, but, however recognised as a modern reality, it doesn't affect the main argument here – that men and women are basically formed so that they may come together as one in order to make more men and women.

There is a growing theology of the body that is wholly directed to under-standing better the total nature of a person. It postulates that humanity was created initially as one body in the image of God, and that this comprises both male and female as one creation. Becoming earthbound, and evolving naturally, the now separated bodies therefore only make sense in relation to each other. We become one again in the act of love. This natural union, the almost inevitable coming together, has a vital importance, because it is this alone that creates life. Scientists may do what they may in their labo-ratories, but the fundamental spark is still exclusive to the original source.

All that really keeps us humans apart are words, language. We all speak differently and, for the most part, incomprehensibly. Yet words are still our best means of communication, even as treasured words give way more and more to internet acronyms, signs and capital letters. Personally, I prefer old-fashioned words that have grown along with humanity itself from the first growl. For that reason, my favourite boyhood reading was the dic-tionary. For me, there was a story behind every entry, and there still is. Most of my professional life has been spent speaking other people's words from a stage. I have taken an even greater pleasure in creating words of my own in books, in each case marshalled for the best effect. I write as they tell me for I believe the right words only obey the right idea. When the spoken word fails, it is better to say nothing. Silence can say much more if left to itself, and, as all lovers know, the body can speak in a language that needs no tongue. On occasion, words fail us and we fall back on instinct and let nature take its course.

What are words anyway, but the wooden foot soldiers of the academic or scholar who arranges them in neat order to do his will while he or she parades their intellect or wide reading, hoping their words might stimulate thought. Even better, words – written, spoken or sung – can create emotion, which is the raw material of love. Emotion, however, flies on its own wings and lands where it will. What we must never forget is that if we really want to find love – and I mean love, not sex – it will find us.

Yes, love is all. It is the only epidemic we all sicken for at one time or another, the one ailment that can do us a power of good. It is the highest common denominator of feeling shared by humans, a powerful medicine whose cost can be great if used carelessly or cruelly, as when it is confused with lust. The only real obstacle to genuine love is ego, which is self-love, therefore contradictory. Love of self is taking in, love of another is giving out. That's why we have words like 'selfishness' and 'selflessness'. The first inhibits, the second inhabits. One is greedy, the other is generous. The marriage partnership is the latter. It is love personified and shared between two, it is their common vocation and strong stuff to be used carefully. Unwise love can distort just as good love reveals. When it is good, we thank our lucky stars and when it's not so good, we have to keep working at it. True love, if left to its own devices, will prevail in all cases.

It's good to love, but better to be loved, especially if we've earned it. It is one of the luxuries of being, but it is easily bruised when handled badly. However, it is almost impossible to kill if it has taken root. Whatever the cynics or pragmatists say, it is still the foremost human need, and, please God, it will continue to be so. The puzzle is, with so much of it around and freely available, why is the real thing so difficult to find? Which is possibly why humanity is fortunate in having the female of the species predominate in this field. A woman has a vested interest in the process for its natural end culminates in her own body. This is why the female instinctively makes herself attractive to men, to prompt mating. It's in their make-up organically as well as cosmetically, and the same need is shown in their attention to clothes.

Clothes, however, maketh not the man, they merely hide his private parts – but a woman's garments can decorate her form and, hopefully, make her even more enticing to everyone and therefore, pleasing to herself. Beauty in either sex comes in all shapes and sizes and in the end, it's all a matter of taste – or chemistry. She makes herself beautiful as he strives to be handsome. Indeed, men today work as hard as women on their appearance and, in any case, they have their own problems. Such as when his voice breaks and his boy soprano tones struggle with the baritone, and even worse when an erection arrives from nowhere. A sturdy libido helps in both cases.

Thinking of the flesh of someone can arouse a sexual response, but if we can see the eyes of that person and see it with our own mind's eye, it makes us want to love them. In the sex act the man gives and the woman takes and both benefit, but it has to be remembered that women pay a large price for being female. When very young they learn about menstruation and the need to wear a towel every month. Then, after puberty follows the agony of childbirth and, in later life, comes the uncertainties of the menopause. And we call them the fair sex. Is it fair that her sex has all this to deal with while the man appears to get off lightly with a few pimples on his face? If Eve really did bring down Adam, it would appear she is still paying for it.

The teenage years are perhaps the most anxious for both male and female because early adolescence is really a time of intense rehearsal for the consummate sexual act to come. Some dread it; others can't wait. For both, it's then a matter of ascending the ladder of love, never missing a rung on the way, because it won't work if either party in the happy conspiracy attempts to take a short cut. The first step is smell. This is the basic animal attraction, although we may be hardly aware of it. The next is touch, a tactile exploration that tells so much of both parties in the early stages. A definite aid to attraction is the blush. For all our advanced communicative technology, the blush is still the first and the best initial signal between interested parties. It is an immediate visual alert from the body and it demands to be answered.

This action, with a bit of luck, soon develops into an easy mutuality, much greater than infatuation. It then becomes a total trust, which leads to unity and on to a complete togetherness that culminates in *oneness* – the top of the love ladder. Marriage or a permanent partnership usually follows.

Marriage may be in decline in our time and partnerships more common, but the pairing of the sexes is still the greatest benefit that can befall a man or woman, because it carries the deepest duty and responsibility – which, in the majority of cases, is to mate and bring another person into the world. Even same-sex couples acknowledge this natural propensity for parenthood by adopting children.

As I have maintained, making a baby is a natural function for the female and male in tandem. It is what their gender dictates. It is their very differences that come together to make the whole. The woman's place in this is almost holy, because what she is asked to do in giving birth is to replicate, more or less, seismic, cosmic action within her own person. From similar small beginnings huge events occur, not in outer space this time but in the inner recesses of the female anatomy. No dark mass this time, but a dark womb where, safely sheltered, the male seed takes root among swirling atoms. From an infinitesimal packet of matter this gradually becomes a small package, which over the given nine months becomes a large package then a very bulky bundle which becomes too big for its enclosed space and forces its way out via the only exit possible. It's a very big parcel for a very small letterbox. The term 'delivery' is more than apt for the process. But the pain felt by this postmistress-mother is just as unimaginable as any Big Bang. It is just as much an explosion in its own way, for it sends into the living world not just the mound of flesh, as we all are at our inception, but a piece of priceless living matter.

Procreation is considered our first duty to our race. Sex, however, is a non-productive act – it is a social pleasure. The fact that sexual contact is a thrill to some is the very reason it is anathema to others who hold it, even today, as something unclean and sinful. But then we human beings are nothing if not variable. It is hard to imagine that a tiny thumbnail of a being that we all once were lived for months in the flesh and bone home especially provided for him or her within the body of the expectant mother until such times as eviction is called for.

What must it feel like to be thrust out of a comfortable darkness into the light and air? I got some idea of how it might be when I delivered my own second daughter. Hers was what they call a torpedo birth. The little darling came flying out with a velocity that took my wife, and me, aback that autumn evening in the upstairs bedroom of our first house in Berkshire. The midwife had been delayed by a car mishap, so with the aid of Dr Spock's notes pinned to the wardrobe door and helped by my wife's instructions, whispered between yelps of pain, I made my rugby catch of the emerging ball of life, and our second child was safely born and lifted high. Within an hour of her arrival she announced her presence with a delightful little snore from the Moses basket in the corner.

From what I have personally witnessed in marriage as a husband and father, being a mother is a lifetime calling. It will last as long as she or the child lives, and until the child has a baby herself, but at this post-natal moment the mother is only happy that her offspring has all its fingers and toes and she gladly takes it to the breast to give it suck. Neither is the prettiest of sights but neither cares. We can only imagine the infant's feelings, thrust out so dramatically from its cellular Eden. Wet, cold and miserable with eyes tight shut, all it wanted to know was that it could go on sucking at that lovely, soft, warm breast. We are in love with our mother already. She, for her part, is only aware that she has just survived her first day in the most important occupation in the world, motherhood.

No matter who she may be, whatever great things she is known for, or achieved, she will never do anything greater than what she has just done in giving birth. She has made another whole being, a completely new person. It is a product of nature, an extension of herself, a symbol of love, nothing less than a small miracle. Who knows what this brand new human will achieve? But does that matter? The miracle here is that mother and child have conspired in an event that is, in human terms, as big as the world. It is the world, as it is now and has it always has been.

There is nothing that we know of worth today that the ancients did not know – at least in the matter of being born of man out of woman. Terence, the Roman playwright, said, 'I am a man: I consider nothing that is human to be alien to me.' He knew the importance of being comfortable in his skin, but the new father hardly feels that. At the birth, if he is there, he stands, looking on, wondering if it's alright to remove the mouth mask he has been wearing. He has probably been in the maternity hospital all day and most of the night, awaiting the big event. Now he is tired, hungry, unshaven and has never felt so useless in his life, but he has never loved his partner in the enterprise more. He is a helpless spectator in this woman's world of perspiration, pain, blood and noise but he takes all the handshakes numbly and trusts that the midwife didn't notice his crying. What has utterly caught the father is the realisation that he has achieved what he has been made for. As W.B. Yeats said: 'Myself I must remake.'

Nobody ever asked to be born. Nor do we select our parents. Just as they have to accept what they get, so do we. With a bit of pushing and pulling by both parties, there we are, object achieved. We are now at the end point of our bloodline, stemming all the way from our particular antecedents and ancestors. Everybody's roots go back to our common beginnings. What begins now is probably the best phase of our life, an idyll, and we will not have a single memory of it. We will be cherished, adored, admired, sighed over, fussed over and cosseted without being able to do anything about it. We are totally helpless about being lifted, dressed, wiped clean and milk-fed. It's called infancy and it's something we have to endure, despite the draughts, the noise, the smells, the rub of strange material on our skin, all of which have to be suffered in the interests of surviving.

What do we think of this new scene swirling around us as, wrapped up in swaddling clothes, we look up from the cot at the giants hovering over us? We can see things now, and we certainly have had our eyes opened. We can hear words, but it's all just noise. What does the new baby think? But can it think when it hasn't had time to learn how to? It doesn't know anything, but happily it doesn't know that yet. That must be a blessing, surely? How else can we imagine true innocence?

Every baby born is a question mark that carries its own answer in every part of its being; if its full possibility is realised by the end of its life, there is no better consummation. Whoever we are, whatever we do, wherever life takes us we will always remain, first and foremost, our mother's child. Her mark is on us and in us, and we will carry her sign about our persons all our lives, not only on our faces, but in every part of our being.

We are now out in the world and there to be gaped at. The time has been noted, the date registered and a name given – one that we will have to live with. We have received the first piece of paper with all the appropriate signatures and, even though we have lived safely and securely for nine months in the womb, we are only now officially declared to be *alive*.

We are now what is called a legitimate being. We exist. And we cry because of the confusion of it all. We can't help it because we don't *know*. Is it that we have a premonition of what human life is like? As King Lear said, 'When we are born, we cry that we are come to this great stage of fools.'

I am now looking at my own birth certificate. It's a rather venerable, yellowing document stating time, date and place: '4.45pm on Sunday 16 February 1930, at 38f Buchanan Street, Baillieston, Lanarkshire, Scotland, UK.' My gran's house. I was a Sunday's child – 'bonie and blythe and good and gay.' Aye, that'd be right! What puzzles me though, in looking at it, is why my grandparents aren't given a mention. They had a hand, however indirect, in my being born. They are a lot more pertinent to my being than my father's occupation as 'Motor Driver'.

What is also worth consideration is that exactly the time I made my 'official' entry into the world, millions of similar births would have occurred and babies of every colour and condition, rich and poor, healthy and not so, of every possible religious background – a vast universe of global birth-time relations – came into being with me. It may be an interesting experiment to post our own birth time and date online. We might find millions of what we could call our global time-siblings. After all, there are nearly seven billion people in more than 200 countries in the world. Surely one is our time-twin? Our 'birth-alikes' might be anywhere in all of this, some just up the road, others on the far side of the world. Wherever they are, they are our virtual extended family. The inner core family is a unit, the extended family a regiment in support and when one adds the close friends that accrete around the doors, the result is a formidable army of kin and kind. We are never alone in a family. But then, nobody should ever be alone in the world. Loneliness is antithetical to our basic social condition.

There is no natural difference between mothers or fathers or babies in any land. Why then are some babies born with everything and others with nothing, or very little? This is the lottery that belongs only to the accident of place and station and does not detract from the fact that this event, like death, is the only time the human is the equal of all. It will be a handful of innocent years before he or she gets an idea of where they stand in the pecking order. It is not something they deduce, but a rude fact that is soon pointed out. Until then, the babe has only one thing to do – grow. Both parents will remember this particular birth day as well as their own, but how much of this will the baby remember?

Memory is the last faculty to develop within us at our beginnings and the first to decay when we approach our end – our second childhood, when everything begins to deteriorate. Memory is first and foremost, an aid, and is there as an additional survival tool. Without memory there could not be foresight. By saving up our experiences for further reference, it serves as a warning system offering a historical self-knowledge that is a guide towards future professional action. Memory is much more than an alternative diary or mere record of events, it is an ongoing faculty to be used when required, not only to look back but to look forward. Using it, we can confidently imagine what might be. Although, if we really knew what was going to happen with absolute certainty, would that not spoil the present and deny us the thrill of discovery?

Ingenuity and foresight are only two of the benefits gained by the use of memory, but these are more the requirements of our striving, later years than the blissful span of early childhood. Imagination is a close cousin of memory, but there is only a family resemblance. Intuition is altogether more elusive and is more a sense than a given faculty, but we all have it to a degree. Memory is more muscular than sensitive. It has both feet on the ground and is ready to spring into action at any time. Names, for instance, are excellent memory triggers. We hear a name and immediately see a face or a place associated with that name. There's no need to imagine it, it comes ready-made with the memory. Anyway, imagination is inclined to soar at times and exaggerate or minimise as the mood takes it.

There are factors in any child's development that are echoed in everyone's growing up. Memories such as these provide can be called on by the user to make assessment of any current situation or assist a judgement on any future course of activity. Scientists call this 'mental time travel', but of course they have to find a name for everything in order to record and codify the ever-accumulating sum of factual information. Knowledge is a different thing altogether. It is often that which comes from the interior of our being rather than that which is imparted externally. This is why we have the savants and the autodidacts, who are self-taught and have only memory and intuition as educational assists. These natural scholars are vital implements in understanding our relation to being because they arrive at their knowledge, not from books or instruction but, intuitively, from a mysterious source within themselves.

Everything comes from within, when you think about it. Like so much in life it has all to do with brain cells, neurons in the brain that are ignited when stimulated. This allows the subconscious to summon the conscious, which provides the picture in our minds that we can see. That is how all memories are utilised. It is not quite a camera, however, for the picture changes over the years due to what is called epigenetic change, or what we call memory loss or memory wear and tear. Birds and bees may have the same problem but they always find their way back to the nest and the hive, as pigeons do to the dovecot – and remember, elephants never forget.

Whether looking backwards, forwards or sideways, our personal narratives are central to our understanding of life and therefore a hint as to our real identity. This underlines the place of memory as a primary aid in our basic function and that's as true of our most recent memory as it is of our first. It is an animal function, as are so many of our human attributes, and we would do well to remember that, at root, that's all we are, refined animals – at times, regrettably, not so refined.

We exist in the actual moment of catching life on the breath – drinking it all in, savouring it, relishing it from first breath to last. It is this elementary act, and nothing more, that gives us our basic taste for existence.

First Interval

The Virtuous Student

My mother told me not to smoke,
I don't.
Or listen to a dirty joke,
I don't.
It was made clear I mustn't think
About intoxicating drink,
I don't.

I was warned to avoid wine, women and song,
I did.
When I thought it might be wrong,
I hid.
I never got to kiss a girl, not one.
I don't even know yet how it's done,
And if you think I don't have much fun,
I DON'T!

CHAPTER TWO

Childhood

Aye be happy leevin', y'er a lang time deid.

OLD SCOTS PROVERB

WE DRAW THE colours from the common human palette and paint our own story on the canvas that is each individual life. We mix the colours as we like – the triumphs, the disappointments, the joys and fondest hopes in all their different tones – and so create the picture of a life as it was lived at a particular time by the person we were then. From the foetus to the womb to the baby at birth and on to the end as the corpse in the coffin is the greatest journey we can take in life, not in terms of time taken, or distance run or things accomplished, but in the quality of existence we have experienced. All through evolution, the driving force has been the need to survive, and where possible, better the human condition. Unfortunately, human beings, being human, tend to get in the way of their own development by petty considerations like selfish ambition, material greed or sheer laziness.

Despite these natural failings, the hope still persists that each generation will be better than the last, but the truth is that humanity still trundles along, replicating itself in its own image and leaving it at that without trying to reconfigure the mould and thus challenge the complacency that so often inhibits or smothers the innate capabilities that lie at our very core. Meantime, we have to co-exist with our fellow beings. Human relationships lie at the root of any civilisation and every recurring mass action stems from how one person deals with another. A simple misunderstanding between a pair of particular people somewhere can lead to a general catastrophe anywhere, as one thing leads to another.

Such large thoughts are not those, however, of the new parents. They know only the elation felt in the safe arrival of a son or daughter. Soon, the milk diet is exchanged for solids, and the child has found two legs to stand on and two hands to get into mischief. The open door beckons and the wee one can just reach the handle. It is the child's first temptation, and the initial drunken baby step is taken on the exploration path that will lead the, hopefully, long way to his or her tomb. But at this stage, the child is only aware that it is a big step for small, shaky legs.

Until now, he or she has owned her own baby-space even when unable to move from it. The slightest whimper is a cue for maternal action, but as soon as the infant finds it has legs, a safe immobility is exchanged for a walking freedom, which, at best, is a risk. Small wonder some babies seem reluctant to toddle. By the time the new he or she can stand on their own two feet and make sounds that resemble words, they become the little prince or princess of a principality that extends from the cot to the front door.

Even when they are taken beyond it into the outside world, they'll be in a carriage and will expect the same royal tribute from utter strangers. They live in a wonderland called Toddlerville where everything is meticulously arranged for their pleasure and comfort, especially if they are the first child. The whole process is called being 'spoiled'. There is no greater tyrant than the two-year-old and in this quarter of life he and she soon learn to make their presence felt. Their power is wielded ruthlessly, but no real harm is done, for the child will remember nothing of it.

Just as fortunately, the growing infant has no sense whatever of the outside world. Its awareness extends only to what it knows in the home environment. Yet, let the mother, and to a lesser degree, the father, be affected by any great worry or anxiety, then that child will pick up that vibration. Its antennae are tuned to detect such atmospheric activity within its given kingdom of the moment. Small happenings around the house are earthquakes to infants. And neither do they pass the nursing mother by.

She has her immediate priorities and all of them are centred on this complicated little person she has brought into her life and into her home. It's a matter of proportionate appraisal. Her offspring learn the importance of being the baby and plays its part to the hilt. At best, the mother has a supporting role in this comedy of many errors. She hardly has a moment to concentrate on that other place they call the outside world. This, in any case, is viewed through a television screen, or ingenious versions of that phenomenon that allow us to watch what is going on with the minority of people while the majority look on. Very soon, living will be nothing more than a spectator sport for billions.

If we go on this way we will have no need for legs. We'll roll from the couch to the car seat to the desk or bench or counter and then the dinner table and finally to bed. A dreary, sedentary procession from morning until night, accommodating at every point our dangerous inclination to passivity. Inaction and lack of activity are the real enemies of physical wellbeing today. If we don't use our bodies, the body itself will take its revenge by going on strike, withdrawing legs first, then arms, then the appetite will fail, and so will we with it unless we take every excuse to get up and get moving. We are such a short time living, it's a shame not to use every bit of ourselves while we can still respond. The real joy is to do anything that makes us say by night time – 'Where did the day go?'

Living is about discovering things, just as children do. The child learns by watching, then copying and repeating. His most valuable aid is his eye. He only knows what he sees, even if he doesn't understand the why of it as yet. Even as we age and grow older, if we keep our eyes open, we'd be amazed at what we see. Better seeing is better being. So much of what we live by is unseen. We have two senses of vision and use both. One is for the immediate, personal, domestic scene around us, the other for those events outside in the world that are beyond our responsibility or understanding, but which, nonetheless, impinge on our conditions of living.

Hence our need to keep aware of things, even when they are invisible. Just because we can't see something doesn't mean it doesn't exist. Momentum, for instance, exists by feeling it, just as we know that other feelings live in us all the time, waiting to be utilised, like love and hate, envy and suspicion, pride – and prejudice. We have also to trust our ability to recognise feelings. They are often our best direction finders – the satellite navigation of the body machine. It pays to listen to our feelings, especially at moments of high tension, but yet not be completely bullied by them either.

Once again, it's in finding the right balance between heart and brain. That is the secret. We are all born with a brain, but how it develops depends on how we use it. It is not always easy to work, and it is difficult to attain a maximum response from it in every situation, but if our body allows us to stand up, sit down, walk and walk fast, run, eat, sleep, talk, and, even better, sing, it is doing all we ask of it and we should be grateful. The extra privilege is in exercising the ability to create. Even if we are not artists, we still have the artistic flair, even if it is only in arranging flowers or furniture. Everything we have in our physical being is there to be used. Experience is the principle item in the survival kit and everyone accrues it on a daily basis whether they realise or not. All one has to do is to acknowledge that the string of days that we hang around our shoulders is proof to everyone that we are of the world and in it – up to our necks.

Charles Edouard Jeanneret, otherwise known as Le Corbusier, the Swiss-born architect, called the house 'a machine for living', but so is the human body. The top of the skull is the roof, the brain is the attic/study where the thinking is done, the chest the reception area where the heart reaches out to friends and strangers. The stomach is the kitchen/dining room, and the gut the pantry where the basics are attended to and from where entry is made to the lower basement between the thighs where the gear is kept to allow the sanitary functions that keep us healthy and may also be used for purposes fully discussed in the previous chapter. Hair is for heating, and eyes the little windows we have to the outside. But windows are also for looking in. Look into anyone's eyes – there's a message there, it can be read, but we rarely look. It's much too invasive, which is why we often talk to each other's noses. Ears are the radio stations, for listening, and arms and legs are only there for lifting or standing or moving to another place.

So much for the body house. Whatever its condition, it's a positive miracle of planning and design. And one of its prime faculties is a unique ability to remember things. In other words, to store up experience. No event can be bigger than life itself, but certain events emerge like torches along the route, highlighting our life journey so far. A first memory is such a thing. It is something we all have in our head, like an excerpt from an old film, and usually dates from no earlier than three or four years of age. However, some people claim to remember actual incidents from their very infancy. This is rare. Most memories are what our mothers or some near relatives have told us. It's amazing what passes for truth in family hearsay.

For instance, an aunt told me that as a baby I used to be sat up in the corner of a big armchair facing the breadbin, which was on a sideboard beside a cathedral-shaped wireless set. Apparently, I stared solidly at the breadbin for hours, but all I remember now is that the bin had a chip out of the letter 'B'.

I've seen a picture of myself as a baby and I look exactly like a little bundle of white wool with big dark eyes. What were those eyes seeing? Could I hear anything under all that wool? Nursery photos ought to be looked at more closely. They tell us not so much of what we were like as infants but how much we were like every other baby in the world, and, in so many respects, still are. I am a long way from my own infancy and I have seen the hawser that tied me to my antecedents gradually slim to a slender rope, then a piece of string, and latterly, a thread – but, astonishingly, it still holds. Strongly.

Yes, early memories are deeply ingrained. What's the very first thing you remember? An image should come to mind immediately. We don't even need to think about it. Where is that little child who once was, no, who still *is*, you? When and where did you take that first step? How long was it before you reached up to the door handle and opened it on to the world? I can only assume, for my own part, that it was in my mother's house and was done with her eye on me. Yet what momentous events such things must have been in that home circle: watching the life machine get under way, its engine starting up.

Everything begins and ends with self and its awareness at all times of being part of the whole. But when are we first aware of self-identity? It can't be in infancy because we don't know enough to dabble in introspection. It is only later, in toddler time, when we come out into the world and see that there are other midgets just like us, but they are all different in some way. They have different hair, different clothes, different voices, and different smells; and yet they behave the same as we do and expect to get their own way, just as we do. In which case, why are there not more serious upsets among the children when they come together in the pre-school nursery?

Young children don't notice colour difference in other children, nor whether the other child is better dressed. They accept what they see and go with it. The only differences arise when it comes to who has a particular toy at the time. A sense of personal property grows as the child does. Who has the toy has the best game still applies in the big wide world. In our early days there is a total lack of that damaging devil, self-pretence. Innocence, in the literal sense, is meeting its first challenge and the child among his peers is forced very early to make adjustments in the interest of building what is called character. The first building bricks are laid here and the German writer Thomas Mann was well aware of this. He wrote in his *Dr Faustus*:

> No biography, no depiction of growth and development... could properly be written without taking its subject back to the pupil stage, to his beginnings in life... when he listened, learned, divined, gazed and ranged, now afar, now close at hand.

The Roman Catholic Jesuit order expresses something of the same spirit in the maxim, 'Give me the child for the first seven years and I will show you the man.' How we end up in life has much to do with how we start. Is the fuel of ambition set in early? What was it first inspired or challenged us, what was it gave us hope and how did we eventually come to the knowledge that anything might be possible?

For many of us, it all started with that first day at school. Some children are taken to school, some are taken by it. I was in the latter category. I *loved* infant school in the East End of Glasgow. Apparently, I had to be dragged away at the end of my first day there. I was so overwhelmed by all the toys available in the first infant class playroom that I wouldn't get off the rocking horse. It took both the janitor and the headmistress to drag me off it and close the school for the day.

Perhaps what fascinated me was all the colour – the bright reds, yellows and blues of the equipment and the sheer size of the rocking horse. This infant escape place had an exotic quality that I never saw in our room and kitchen in a grey stone tenement. Not that we ever had any complaints about where we lived. We were never cold, or hungry or unloved, but comfortably clothed, well fed and our interest maintained at all times. It was crowded, but that was tenement living, and we were more than happy with that. It was all we knew, but I didn't know about colour until school happened.

It was in the same huddle of little wooden huts under the shadow of the Irn-Bru factory that I was to meet my first mentor, a spinster school-teacher, typical of her era, who took her gang of boy and girl puppets on a word journey over the next five years that stretched the strings that tied them together, as well as to her. By dint of sheer application she transformed many of them into grammar school pupils and even future schoolteachers. Others, of course, served time in other directions, but they were in the minority. Schooling opened so many doors and windows to me, not only at primary school, but in my head. The door led into the school and the school let me see out of the windows in my mind.

It was school that first made sense of the world to me and introduced that other, better world: books. That wonderful universe of the imagination, for which I was to hold a lifetime passport. No boy could have been given a better introduction to schooldays – the first decade of which did indeed contain some of the happiest days of my life. I quickly learned the importance of reading and only slightly less, that of writing. Given the ability to read, we can educate ourselves – as many did. I knew one man in the East End who, during the Depression and jobless, went every afternoon to the local library and read through *The Encyclopaedia Britannica* from start to finish. The same kind of self-schooling is something that has continued for me throughout my life, but once I was able to write I was able to communicate, even at a rudimentary level.

This was my primary teacher's credo: that her pupils should first be able to communicate. Whether by talking or writing was no matter, as long as they made their meaning clear. It was a good lesson at an age when we soak up information greedily. Our first mentor knew this and thrust its importance on us with all the force of a fanatic. So much so, that I have gone through life with a book at the bedside, wherever I am, and a notebook and pen at the ready, just in case. I have so much to thank Miss Susan Callaghan for. From her, I learned that education was a very individual exercise. As she said, she would take us to the window, but it was up to us to describe the view.

In short, we had to show some intellectual initiative. We were there to learn how to learn and from then on it was up to each one of us to decide how earnestly we applied ourselves. I got into books as soon as I could. I read anything in print, even instructions on public notices. I remember thinking that 'Trespassers will be Prosecuted' meant that they would be executed! I joined the local public library and was soon borrowing two books a week. When, later on, I delivered newspapers around the tenements, I read most of them before shoving them through the various letterboxes. A sentence from a wartime *Daily Express* is still in my head to this day: 'Round the powdered shoulder of the ben, the black limousine came like a black stranger into the white world of snow…'

It was written by a wonderful journalist called James Cameron and it dealt with the visit to Scotland of Mr Avril Harriman, President Roosevelt's representative, who was on his way to a secret meeting with Prime Minister Winston Churchill in a Glasgow hotel. And here was a little boy in short trousers sitting on the stone stairs reading about it in a newspaper, speaking it aloud to himself just for the pleasure of it. Gathering knowledge of anything is an adventure and children are naturally drawn to it. It's all part of the search that childhood is, and the outbreak of the Second World War in 1939 was, for a boy, as big an adventure as he could get. If we are going to be in a war at all, it's better to be in it between the ages of nine and fifteen and well removed from the action.

A world war completely coloured my childhood, although, ironically, it was largely black and white. It had, however, the same effect that the world's economic depression had on my parents' generation in the 1930s and the First World War had on my grandparents before that, and again, the Boer War on my great-grandparents at the turn of the century. It is always the large, outside events that shape ordinary lives far removed from the decision makers. It's like firing a gun in the North Pole and the bullet ricochets off Ben Nevis and hits somebody in Piccadilly Circus.

War is a large event far removed from ordinary people on the lower rungs in every country, yet it affects everyone at every level to some extent, even fatally. Imperial wars were always echoes of what had gone before. The Boer War duplicated Waterloo, the First World War repeated the ideals of Mafeking, the Second World War was really the continuation of the First but then the atom bomb changed all the rules in 1945. However, in 1939, the whole of Britain was endangered because of one politician's loyalty to a piece of paper but was saved by another's gift for jingoistic rhetoric.

In many ways, the war machines are still kept at the ready today even if it is on a more sophisticated, scientific level in laboratories and not on battlefields. In our time, a button can be pressed a thousand miles away and do more damage and cost more lives than a machine gun ever did from a trench. As the Chinese saying has it, 'the reputations of generals are built on the dead bodies of 10,000 men.' Bullets are profitable because all wars anywhere are moneymakers for some and disasters for the rest of us. Pacifists are always the poorer, but humanity itself would be the poorer without them.

All I knew as a ten-year-old boy was that war was unreal. It was something that happened on the wireless and it was hard to believe that people we knew were being killed as they slept in their houses only because they didn't want to spend the night in a concrete shelter below ground. The bombing got worse, so they sent all children into the countryside. It was called evacuation and what a life trauma that was, the city street exchanged for the farmyard. My genes hadn't prepared me for such a change. My DNA was totally antithetical to any rural atmosphere. How then did I cope as a child?

It was easy, because it was all too strange to be true. How did my mother manage? Waving her two sons away on a train as she did, not knowing where they were going? She was aware, too, that her husband was enduring the London Blitz, having been conscripted into the Ministry of Works as the foreman of a rescue team. She herself had to work in an ammunitions factory. My mother had no option. There was a war on, she was told. We were constantly reminded of that by posters that said things like 'Keep Calm and Carry On!' Most did, but some neighbours were imprisoned for protesting publicly about the war and were sent to prison. People soon learned to shut up. All my poor mother learned from the war was how to smoke. Every adult seemed to smoke then.

There was a shortage of everything except humour. Whatever the circumstances, ordinary people can nearly always find a laugh, but chocolate was rationed and yes, we had no bananas. Austerity was no bad thing. The enforced Spartan diet did us no harm. We could appreciate what we had and not what we were missing, and more than anything we learned there was so much we could do without. The ration book was suddenly our passport to better health, but the paper scarcity meant that new books were few and I was now far from a library – but the Cairney brothers landed lucky. We had a completely aristocratic time of it.

Jim and I were billeted first with Sir Malcolm and Lady Campbell in their mansion house near Gretna on the Scottish side of the English border. Then the 'Phoney War' ended and we were returned home. When the bombs started dropping we were sent off again, this time to Prime Minister Neville Chamberlain's holiday home in Kinloch Rannoch near Pitlochry. I was having a very upper-class war. This was underlined when I was moved on my own to the Earl of Cluny's mansion in order to attended secondary school at Aberfeldy Academy. I saw a grand piano for the first time and learned what knife and fork to use at the dinner table. This remarkable period in my nine- to 12-year-old phase couldn't have given me a better education – at least in social experience. I was being spoiled again.

No wonder I came back to the tenement more than a little ill-adjusted. It was abruptly brought to an end by events that brought home to me the knowledge that I still belonged to dear, old Glasgow. Without even an air raid warning, I was catapulted back home on orders from someone. That was how things happened in wartime.

Overnight, the gangling boy that I now was had to reconcile himself to a room and kitchen after his mansion-house year in the countryside. How small our house seemed. I had been away long enough to have grown used to the good life and its generous proportions. My mother was not impressed and made her opinion clear.

'Ye needny act the Lord Muck noo,' she said. 'A room an' kitchen's been good enough for better folk than us, so nane o' yer nonsense.'

I was home again.

I can well imagine, looking back, the shock to the system that this whole evacuation business must have been to a growing boy now returned to his city streets. Parkhead now seemed colourless and restricting. I had grown used to space and a sort of privileged freedom. And fresh air – lots of it. Now I was back in that 'dear, green place', but really Glasgow was all steam, smoke and soot, and readjusting was difficult. My sense of being had been badly disturbed and I needed to reorientate.

What saved me was my new school, St Mungo's Academy, a Catholic boys' school in Townhead, a tram ride away, and Glasgow Celtic Football Club, which was just across the road. They were surely the worst team in the Scottish Football League at the time, but the chalice had been passed down and I drank of it deeply. I queued up with the rest of the tykes at the sevenpenny gate and found that colour was again restored to my life, and it was solidly green and white. It didn't matter that our team never won. The enthusiasm was all. Over the next couple of years, as I moved from junior to senior school and began to mix with the big boys, I was fully blooded into the mystical rite of supporting a football club and the passion it demands. Once initiated, it is a loyalty that never leaves you.

My whole being was totally focused on the strip of green grass called Celtic Park, where my elected heroes pranced about with a football, bringing a much-needed romance into my sombre tenement life. This was a real love experience. I stood huddled among an army of grey coats and flat caps, feeling my heart thud from the moment the teams came out on to the pitch. The excitement I felt when the whistle blew to start the match I still felt as it blew to end it. What did it matter that we had lost again. For 90 minutes I had hardly breathed in my new, other world of possibility. Oh yes, there was a time when this sport called football was so much more than a game, but you had to be 12 to realise that.

It was around then I had my first ever journey alone into the foreign land of England and to the new stranger in my life, my own father. I hadn't seen him for years, although I had the happiest memories of him. His smile, his easy chat, his piano playing, his reading of books that were beyond me, his almost dapper dress sense that reminded me he was a band leader in his younger years. How, on the family's annual holiday in Ayr, he swam in the sea and once carried me out on his back until I was clinging on, terrified. How he seemed to know every star in the sky, and pointed them out to Jim and me on clear nights. He told us there was a star up there for each of us. I remember asking him to point out mine. He said he couldn't, I had to find my own. I asked where his was. He said he lost it years ago when he gave up the pipe band for the dance band. He wouldn't say anymore. That was my father.

Now here he was, waiting for me at the ticket gate in Euston, looking as smart as ever in suit and tie and holding his arms out wide as I ran to him to be engulfed in a warm, tight embrace. That was the first time my father had ever hugged me, and I think it was the last. The father and son relationship is not an easy one. Of course we loved each other, but we never said so, or showed it openly. It was not at all like the relationship a son has with his mother. He can hug her every five minutes and argue with her in between. I never argued with my father. I listened to him and enjoyed it. He was a trim gas heater to my mother's open coal-fire blaze. They both gave out warmth, but one was controlled by a switch and the other was a messy, haphazard, ever-changing flame that danced with the heat of a furnace but never went out. Which is why I could burn my fingers on her at times, but Dad was safe because he was encased in tartan plaid.

In our London time I knew I had a real chance to get near him, but I never did.

Of course, he had work to do, and dangerous work at that, but he gave me all the time he could, which was only in the afternoons, as he had to be available at night when the air raids began. It was an absolutely fascinating time for me, nonetheless, and I'm so sorry that my London has long gone. It was dirty, dishevelled and damaged by bombs and fire, but I can only remember chirpy Cockney voices – it was still their London – polished Earl of Cluny accents in the City and everything in between. There was a palpable spirit about the place, a defiance that belonged to a castle under siege and, most of all, an inter-concern that linked them all like a family making the best of things. For the moment, I felt that my father was part of that family, not mine. He strolled through it all as if he belonged to the place.

My admiration for him grew hourly, but I so wanted to *love* him. However, I could only feel a kind of distance between us, probably my fault. He was a great talker and I was a ready audience. I told him I still remembered him practising his pipe band music at the kitchen table with his chanter. I remembered he played it so softly, like a clarinet. 'Aye, right enough, son. But I never could get the snake to come out of the sauce bottle,' he said with a twinkle. He was lovely company at these times, but somehow I always felt he was hiding himself in the performance and keeping me, his own son, at arm's length. He was an authority on lots of things and even when he wasn't, he still talked as if he was, and the unbelievable Blitz time, so ghastly for so many, for us flew by.

When I watched at night-time from the window in Water Lane, Brixton, with a pillow over my head, I gazed in wonder at the white searchlights stabbing at the red sky above the smoke and fires and listened to the noise of screeching ambulances, anti-aircraft guns and German planes overhead, not to mention the sound of bombs falling and exploding in the streets. Poor Londoners. I felt removed from them, as if I were watching a film. It was all so unreal, I couldn't really take it in. My own father was down there in the middle of it all, doing what he had to do. There was a war on. And this was it. He was a hero and I was proud of him. But then, isn't every father a hero to his son? All the same, I wished he had talked about my mother more.

On my return to Glasgow, to my real dismay, I found that schooldays at St Mungo's were becoming boring. This was not the fault of the Marist Brothers or of the other staff, many of whom I'm sure felt the same, but just got on with it. I felt off-balance and it showed in my erratic attendance record and no application to study whatsoever. The London week had shaken me and I tried to read it off, but it was all the wrong stuff – Proust, Joyce, Eliot, etc. One result of this very personal agenda was that I left school. I didn't do so officially. One day I just didn't go back. Something told me that my happy, if slightly chequered, childhood was over.

I was tired of being churned up inside. It was mere body matter, I suppose – growing pains or something. It came with the pimples and blackheads, but I couldn't get over the feeling that my boots were now too big for me and my cap no longer fitted my big head. It was swelling with ideas, but hormones were screeching all over my insides, all yelling different orders, and I never knew what to listen to or in which direction to turn. Sex had reared its pretty head and I began looking more closely at girl's breasts, but this was noticed only by the subsequent reaction in a hitherto insignificant part of my anatomy.

At nights in bed I often thought of my poor old dad still on his English 'Foreign Service'. I really loved him now and I missed him. Did he miss us, I wondered? What a shame he had lost his star. I couldn't see mine because of the blackout curtains. It was time to sleep.

Second Interval

Dae Ye Mind?

Dae ye mind when the sun seemed to shine a' day
An' nights were storybook long?
An' ye made shadow fancies
Oan the plaster wa' o' the bed
'til you were feart o' your ain imagination,
But ye fell asleep afore the big monster got ye
An' ye minded nothin' 'til the mornin'.

Dae ye mind how ye woke fresh as toothpaste
Eager tae brush wi' the day?
That stretched afore ye like a rimless desert
Dotted wi' mealtimes
An' unexpected oases
Tae see somethin', take a breather,
Even a breath.

Dae ye mind when life wis sae big a thing
Ye never even thought about it?
An' if ye did
It wis only tae giggle aboot how easy it all was.
Now ye've grown up
An' the world has shrunk a wee bit,
Takin' its simplicity wi' it.
Leavin' ye tae fathom the complexities
On its tired, auld face.

Your eyesight's not so good,
Ruined by politic short-sightedness,
The need tae see everythin' ye have to see,
Missing everything essential
In your desperation to miss nothing.
Dae ye mind when ye understood nothing?
An' ye see now, it was a gift,
An' ye threw it away!
Dae ye mind?

CHAPTER THREE

Adolescence

*Life can only be understood backwards; but it must be lived
forwards.*

SØREN KIERKEGAARD

THE RISING OF THE sun in the morning is a signal of hope. It tells us that
we can all start anew, refreshed, rested and eager for the day. The sun is
not just the life-giver to the globe, it is also, or should be, the flame that
fires our body impulses and gets us going. Each succeeding day tells us
that all our yesterdays are dead and tomorrow is yet to be born. As the
Buddhists say, 'Tomorrow is another world.' It's not here yet, so concentrate on the whole, new, bright day that awaits with a glass of orange juice
or cup of tea. Why not look on each new dawn as a friend? There's no
need to grab for it, it's there for the taking. Each day is there to be lived
as if it were the rest of our life. We should be curious about what might
happen. What will we remember of it? What will we try to forget? Who
knows what will happen? We should be excited.

We learn most about life by actually living it. There are no end of term
breaks in the life academy, nor long summer vacations. The learning rolls
on and on without stop. It is available in full measure to those who drill
deep enough to find out its many possibilities. We must pay attention to
what life is constantly trying to tell us. This relies on the individual's
knowing, or trying to find out, what he or she is capable of doing and
applying it forcefully to the appropriate option as it presents itself.

Mental muscle matters as much as the physical ability to keep going. If
we store up as much mind matter as leg muscle we'll be fit for any journey.
After all, our limbs don't move of themselves. They have to be told what
to do. So we tell them. And we have to make sure they go where we want
them to go. Having set these parameters, we joyfully seize the day.

And what a day was Tuesday, 8 May 1945.

VE Day – Victory in Europe and the 'All Clear' sounded its single-note

55

serenade all over the land, including the tenement rooftops of good old gallus Glasgow. For me, a growing boy, now 15-years-old and still new to long trousers, who followed the bonfires right across his own city from Parkhead Cross to Partick Cross, it was the beginning of a wild, nocturnal progress towards adolescence. I was caught up in the celebrating flames because I was on fire myself. It didn't matter that by day I was a temporary office boy in the Ministry of Food offices in town, I was now making pretensions to be my own man out on the street among the sing-songs, the dancing and the VE street parties that went on all night. They were my inauguration into the good time had by all as that wonderful day became a night to remember.

Not since Britain celebrated Waterloo or Trafalgar in the 19th century, or raised the roof for the Relief of Mafeking at the start of the 20th, was there such immediate and spontaneous celebration. The atom bomb was three months away, but Europe was jumping the gun for peace with all stops pulled out. People – complete strangers to one another – hugged and kissed, danced and sang in the streets because the war was over and they were still alive. Who couldn't be roused by this sudden, uninhibited display of all-round body contact as the lights went on again and the barricades came down? The barricades were not only in the streets, the doors thrown open were also in my awakening physique. The new, peacetime surge of joy that swept through the entire city, also swept this particular man-child or child-man into the choppy waters of puberty.

What was important for me was that the VE Day experience took me out of my own East End streets for a momentous day and showed me the West End streets for the first time. I was in my own city, yet they were two different worlds. In the East End, I was among my own kind and I was easy with it. Up West, they were all kinds and it thrilled me. Yes, as a boy I had the life change of the evacuation, but here was an epiphany lit by bonfires and celebrated by song and laughter, with anything goes in the middle. Just right for a teenager, especially one still an innocent. For me, it was a blitz on my senses and it only lasted for one glorious day and night.

People living in our tense, doubting 21st century will find it hard to understand the sheer happiness that came over Britain in 1945 and the immediate years that followed. The sense of a fresh start was everywhere.

This new vision was shown by the Labour Party as it floated into power on the tidal wave of the returning serviceman vote. Social equality was the latest idea for the age and the times changed to allow it to happen. Ordinary people felt they had got their own country back and a wonderful sense of optimism permeated every level of society. Except for the rooted landowners, of course, and the industrial capitalist cabal, who hoped the current euphoria wouldn't last, as that could mean the end of their dominance. People were telling themselves they had just won a war and surely a new peace would be half the bother. Hopes soared and national morale was high. It was a Great time to be British.

As the '40s inched towards the '50s, I had other challenges to face. After a succession of weekly wage packets, and with my mother's permission, I had the effrontery to have my first suit made, in the best, wide-shouldered bandleader tradition and in an impudent blue at that. I was unashamedly being my father's son, at least in the matter of image. The addition of a Windsor knot in my tie and a pair of smooth Hush Puppies completed the picture of youth on the make. I had no idea what I was on the make for, but I was fully intent on making an impression, much to my mother's annoyance.

Like any apprentice being, I was the happy spectator of my own show-off time. Not being quite sure what was happening to me, but even with my breaking, two-tone voice, I could pretend to be anyone. I was a Polish army officer one week, an American beach boy the next and a disreputable tramp after that. This confused the neighbours and bewildered my mother. She used to cross to the other side of the road when she saw me coming. It may have been this initial attempt to find a new identity that caused me to think of myself in the third person. I wanted to be anybody but me. We hate in others what we see in ourselves, but I was too callow as yet to understand that.

The mirror I held up to nature only reflected the self I regularly changed and presented to the world, but this was the only way I felt I could survive the daily turmoil that every day was. This was being an adolescent. Adolescence is not just another stage in life: it's a condition, a confusion of impulses, and a serious physical and mental derangement – in short, a right mess. It is a further step along the way for the young human, but it's more than just another rung on the development ladder. It affects not only the in-between person concerned, but all those who surround him or her at this extremely vulnerable time. Yet vulnerability is the last trait shown. A swagger is developed to mask the shyness and the loud, often variable voice is raised to hide the timidity. The performance is so obvious that it is a wonder it is accepted, but despite all the annoyance, and often pain it causes to others, the youth perseveres in the act until the years work their own cure and he finally emerges as an adult.

I realise now that in those up and down teenage times I was constantly trying to get away from the boy I still was. I hid in my imagination, which was why I thought it was safer to think of myself as 'he'. I didn't need then to come face-to-face with the sweats, skin rash, dandruff and all those uncomfortable, youthful dreams. This revolt against my own personality was only another symptom of the furore going on in my body, but actually, in many respects, I was having the time of my young life. I couldn't understand why my behaviour was considered such a serious matter. I tried everything, this and that, here and there, now and then, and hoped something possible would emerge. The prospect of sex, for instance, hovered dangerously.

Meantime, I tried to laugh everything off, but the result was often nearer hysteria, because inside (although I hated to admit it), I was now crying tears of genuine misery. Underneath the seemingly arrogant exterior of early adolescence was a very uncertain self. My mother shrewdly guessed this, and told me once that if I was to laugh correctly I had first to learn how to smile.

It's perfectly natural to want to be noticed. Vanity is a good shield when required. We all need to confirm that we are here and now, and recognition is the only reward wanted. It tells the world that we want to participate.

Actually, I was living it to my limit, which, at this stage, wasn't too extensive. Fortunately, two elements combined to offer me the twin door to proper self-expression and eventual fulfilment. One was amateur theatre and the other commercial art, but before that there was an even bigger hurdle to get over for the emergent male – GIRLS.

They were terrifying at first because as far as I could see, as we boys might have a couple of pals, girls went about in packs. I had no sisters or even close female cousins, so I had no experience of them as separate individuals since primary school. I was your genuine innocent and longing to know more, but didn't know how to go about it. I joined the local Catholic Youth Club because of the chance to play billiards, and it was here I met my first girlfriend. She was part of the inevitable group of girls that mixed with my crowd of boys and personal attachments were unavoidable. Some of the boys did indeed marry some of the girls and eventually I was expected to follow suit with this young girl. She was a month older than I was and a steadying influence. At least she put an end to the sartorial experiments. Our initial relationship was puppy love – no more – and like puppies we jumped about, rolled around and occasionally, fell flat on our faces, figuratively speaking. But no harm was done.

If there were feelings at all, they were kept well in control and the whole sequence of first love behaviour in the post-war period followed this pattern exactly. At most, more expressive gestures evolved in the guise of heavy petting and adventurous touch, but in the main, the approach to anything like sex at this time was timid and inhibited. This was not only our mutual instinct, but also a reflection of the culture of the time. Neither of us was in any great hurry. As always, it was an external factor that moved things along in this wavering stage.

While on the badminton court, I was spotted as a possible actor by the young man charged with producing a one-act play for the Glasgow Youth Club Drama Festival. He was planning to do an excerpt from *Julius Caesar* and thought I could play Mark Anthony. 'Why not?' I thought. 'Anything for a laugh.' I was given the scene and started learning the words: 'Friends, Romans, Countrymen …' echoed round the room and kitchen in Williamson St for a week, much to my mother's amusement. At least she was pleased to see that her son seemed genuinely involved.

The other element emerging around this time was art. I had always drawn since chalking wartime aeroplanes on the blackboard at school to amuse my classmates. I had won a gold medal in the 1943 Glasgow Schools Art Competition and the next year got a silver. In a roundabout way, this had got to the ears of the Director of the Art School, possibly via my old art teacher at St Mungo's, Mr Robertson. I was invited to come into the Art School for an interview. I hurriedly concocted a portfolio, which was accepted, and I was in.

I liked the Director of the School immediately, but I didn't like the Art School at all. It may have been a Rennie Mackintosh masterpiece architecturally, but in 1947 it was cold and dark inside because of electricity restrictions, and full of mature students. Men with beards and yellow faces who had been prisoners of war in Japan. They were scary. It was suggested that I should perhaps change over to evening classes until I got used to the stark ambience of the place, and move back to full-time when I felt more relaxed with conditions. I agreed, and that's how I got to know the bust of Julius Caesar. That was all I did for a whole term; draw Julius Caesar with a pencil. This was all the more ironic, because I was now rehearsing to play Mark Anthony: 'I come to bury Caesar, not to praise him...'

The selected scene was duly entered in the Drama Festival and, to my surprise, I was advised by the Adjudicator on the night, Mr Paterson-Whyte, to 'seriously consider a future in the theatre as an actor.' It was the way he said 'ac-tor' that made the impact. It was certainly not something I had ever considered. I had never been in a real theatre, except for the annual family pantomime at the Alhambra, and anyway, I thought you had to be English to be an actor. Or at least, come from Giffnock or Newton Mearns. No one from Parkhead had ever gone on stage, as far as I knew. But then, I didn't know very much about anything, except what I'd read in books.

But what I did know was that what I *wanted* to do I did so thoroughly, and to the exclusion of everything else. If I had been a street sweeper, Glasgow would have had the cleanest streets in Europe. I surrendered immediately to every obsession, believing it had found me. I hadn't been looking for *it*. So far, this had got me nowhere, but I had never guessed that the stage would loom into my sooty horizon. Should I follow it up and see what happens? I wasn't sure.

I similarly wasn't sure if I were really in love with my first girlfriend. I had a good feeling for her, that was for sure – she was a smart, pretty girl. I knew that from the time I helped walk her dog in Tollcross Park and I knew it, too, when I kissed her after seeing her home at nights. At least, it was different from the head-on, closed-lipped, labial collisions I had known at tenement house parties. No, her kisses were soft and tender, undemanding and sweet. It did not go further, but we didn't need to. We were both aware of a warm feeling swirling up between us but unsure about how to deal with it. We also knew, at the same time, that something would happen when the chance came.

It's not that we didn't know what to do, or that we didn't want to do it. The right time will come, we kept telling ourselves. We could wait. She was nubile, and I was the usual teenage mix, all boy-man inside but all man-boy on the outside. That's the way love and desire come to young people, but she and I both knew the time was not yet. Or was it just that we were too Catholic-conditioned to try? What a nuisance the opposite sex is to the 17-year-old male.

I tried to concentrate on my new theatre interest to see if it were a real alternative. Anything was better than sitting around doing nothing and thinking of the impossible. I had been taken up by an amateur group, a lady- and gentleman-like collection of Catholic schoolteachers and publicans with drama leanings, but I felt penned in among them, especially as I was strongly advised by them not to even think of a theatrical career.

'Much too unreliable, and morally doubtful in many cases,' I was told.

Things weren't much better at the Art School. If this was art training, it was dreary. I started to stay away from classes, just as I had done at school, but I used the Art School drawing materials I now possessed to make posters and notices on the kitchen table for pubs, shops and offices in my home area; that old, built-up triangle between Parkhead Cross, Shettleston Cross and Bridgeton Cross. In no time I had a nice little ring of customers at five shillings a time for a shop, ten for a restaurant and a pound for the pubs. I had to fight with my mother for the use of the kitchen table each day to meet the demand. I was even offered a job in a city advertising office. They needed someone to draw ships for the Ellerman Shipping Line, but I didn't want a job. I enjoyed being my own man.

My mother wasn't too pleased. She thought that 'sitting drawing wee pictures wi' coloured pencils' wasn't a real job. I paid her off by giving her half of what I earned, which was sometimes as much as my father did, now returned from England, and, at present, tending a furnace in Parkhead Forge. If puberty is a time of change, then the shuttle-box of hot tinders that was Tom Cairney's son was still incapable of differentiating between mischief and impish adventure. I wanted to be shaken, if only to enjoy the sensation, but I was totally devoid of any serious purpose. I didn't know then that that was what being adolescent was all about. I was hungry for experience but procrastination was undoubtedly my best friend. I was still determinedly star-chasing, but then, as is the way of things, right out of the blue, the drifting, self-employed teenager got the first glimpse of the light his father had talked about.

At a Quiz Night in the Youth Club, I was the only one who knew who that 'The Old Lady of Threadneedle Street' was the nickname of the Bank of England and that snippet of general knowledge won me a pair of stall tickets for *The Righteous Are Bold*, the play then in production at the Citizens Theatre in the Gorbals. Here was my first chance to see real actors in a real play in a real theatre. I couldn't let it pass. I could then see for myself what it meant to be an actor. It all started from that night. There must have been a germ in the posh stall seats, for I caught the theatre bug there and then and the sickness spread until it became a life-threatening illness. I had to do something about it. But how? Or what? How does one get to a stage door from a tenement close in the East End of Glasgow? And in the way of things when they are meant to be, it all seemed to happen fortuitously.

The Marian Players were amateur, but they told me that a semi-professional theatre was active in Rutherglen, just over the Clyde from us, a matter of a few tram stops away. They were looking for actors to add to their pool of players for the new season. It called itself a Repertory Theatre and that was enough for me. I duly reported for an audition. To my surprise, I was taken on, as they needed a young Cockney soldier for their next show. I told them I had been in London for a week when I was 12 and got the part. I was in, just as effortlessly as the Art School. I just hoped Rutherglen didn't have any returned prisoners of war.

I skipped back home over the Clyde and couldn't wait to tell my mother. She thought the idea of her son as a Cockney was daft. His father thought the whole idea of theatre was daft and a spotlight wasn't a starlight, at least not in the sense he had meant it.

'But Dad, it might make *me* a star one day.'

'Oh aye?' was the dry retort.

'Whit does it maitter whit he does? As long as it gets him oot frae under my feet.'

My mother was ever practical.

The best decisions are always made for us by circumstances beyond our control. The worst are always decided after too much thinking about it. Undue delay doesn't belong to good thinking. The answer is nearly always staring us in the face, if only we'd stop staring into the mirror. Maybe I should have looked at the back of my head in the mirror. It might have helped me to see where I was going. Changes come from the inside as much as from the outside. This time, however, I felt I was being carried along on a whole new wave of events and I was quite happy to let myself go with the current. The drifter had found a sudden purpose in an area he appeared to enjoy, and it engulfed everything around him to the detriment of everything else.

I was completely taken up in this new theatrical excitement. Art School was allowed to drift a little and even the kitchen table drawing office closed down temporarily. I was badly shaken by this cocktail of sudden events, but wasn't that what I had wanted? Wasn't this the instinct that was behind all the adolescent posing and pretending, trying to get away from the self, which all the time was trying to tell me what I should be doing with my life.

Meanwhile, I was the round peg who had unexpectedly found a round hole. My whole personality, like my father's, was geared to performance, yet I felt this drive was sustained by an unexpected inner strength gained from a gradual, growing surety. I had been thrashing about in a whirlpool of my own making but, somehow, the waters had settled to this particular thespian channel and I let myself be swept along, knowing I was in no danger of drowning.

This was made even more certain when I was thrown a lifebelt in the shape of an offer of a full professional contract by the Park Theatre, so called because it overlooked the West End Park. Someone had seen me at Rutherglen. I was glad to move from the East End to meet the management and discuss the terms of the contract, which I duly signed on 8 December 1947. To my own amazement, I could now call myself a professional actor. It was an immense milestone. I was cast as the Clown in Marlowe's *Dr Faustus* and Second Old Jew in *Salome* by Oscar Wilde. I wish now that I had made contact with that adjudicator to tell him that I had taken his advice.

The only downturn in this exciting phase was that I had rather lost touch with Parkhead and the other way of life. Of course, I saw the girl-friend as often as rehearsals and performances permitted, but this meant that our stumbling courtship was really confined to long walks on a Sunday or a hurried hour in a café. There was no doubt that we were by now a couple and recognised as such, but a likeable young lady was beginning to look a little neglected. When we met now it was as if we were going through an expected ritual, playing as cast in a play in which neither of us knew how it ended.

'You're bigger than I thought you were,' she said.

'That's because I've started to grow on you!' he answered.

There was no doubt we made a good pair, with everything in common that we needed. All our friends expected an eventual wedding, or an official engagement at least. That seemed the logical outcome, but something made me procrastinate again. Was this fair to her? Or even to me? Instinct told me it wasn't right to do *anything*. But how can anyone know what to do about anything at 18? All I knew at that age was that no matter how illusionary love may be, it wasn't theatre. It doesn't happen on stage, it happens *at* a stage, or successively in stages, in all our lives. It is one of our more primitive responses, almost extremely so, and, for that reason, it can make its presence felt aggressively. We fall into it because we can't help it.

A wedding is not always the outcome, but it is the natural end product. The ceremony is much more than a social custom, it is an age-old edifice built to accommodate two willing parties who agree on its construction and are content to live in it happily ever after. This outcome looked inevitable for us until early in 1948, when another piece of paper came through the letterbox at 20 Williamson Street. It was a Government Order for me to report for a medical examination prior to National Service in the Royal Air Force. This was quite unexpected, or rather ignored, my being then on a happy honeymoon with acting. A theatrical occupation was not held to be grounds for exemption and my status at the Art School was weakened for the same reason – 'absence while on theatrical duties elsewhere'.

There was no option but to attend the medical, and in a matter of weeks, being passed fit, I was given a date to report to the training centre, RAF Padgate, near Warrington in Lancashire.

It meant another train to England, but this time the rail ticket was paid for. But what to do about my now steady young lady? Impulsively, I did what I thought was the right thing – I gave her an engagement ring. We would marry when I completed my two years of National Service. Was this just another delaying tactic? Time would tell. We celebrated by arranging a very daring trip to Edinburgh, ostensibly to sleep together in the same room and get rid of our mutual virginity far from the Parkhead Youth Club. I still don't know how I had the nerve to suggest it or she the character to agree, but she did, and here we were. Unfortunately, in the theatre digs we arranged (with the help of a colleague from the Park Theatre) the tough old landlady insisted we have separate rooms, even though we flaunted the engagement ring. After a whispered agreement with my co-conspirator that I would come down to her on the stroke of midnight, we parted.

'Mind the stairs, there's a creak on them,' she warned me.

As I put on my pyjamas in the upstairs room, I was suddenly so aware they were crisp and brand new. I checked that the price wasn't still on them. I then lay on top of the bedcover and glanced at my watch: ten minutes past eleven. Was that all? Forty minutes to go – almost an hour. I hoped that the landlady was asleep. I yawned but I wasn't in the least tired. I was too excited. I wondered if my girl felt the same. I was almost shy, timid even, about how it all might go. After all, this was a big, first time for both of us. This was it. But *what* was it? I'd soon know. I tried not to think about it and stretched out arms and legs in a swell of antici- pation. Should I say an Act of Contrition now or wait until afterwards? I didn't want to think about that. I drew a deep breath and felt a reaction in that part of my anatomy that would soon be actively involved. I wished I had brought a book but I didn't think I'd need one. I had only one object in view this weekend – no, I mustn't think about it. Just let it all happen in its own time. I closed my eyes but I couldn't stop smiling…

Suddenly, I heard a loud banging on the door, and heard the landlady's voice calling loudly, 'Are ye still in there? Ye'll be late for yer breakfast and the young lassie's waitin' for ye'.

I sat straight up immediately. It was daylight. I had slept through the night! Bloody hell! I jumped out of bed in a panic to find that my new pyjamas were sticky wet in a certain area. I stood there like a fool. What a bloody idiot I was. I felt mortified, sickened, humiliated, yet – yet there was the tiniest whisper of relief. I then burst into tears.

I can't remember much about breakfast, but since it was now Sunday morning we went to Last Mass in St Mary's Cathedral. I still had that strange mixed feeling of relief and guilt. The lustful expedition had petered out lamely. The innocents abroad had returned home, innocent. We both remained *virgins* but were now burdened with all the guilt of sinful intent. Why is it always so awkward to be Catholic? It was almost laughable. So we laughed. What else could we do?

Back in Glasgow, I didn't say anything to anyone about the incident. I was too embarrassed and glad I had been offered an escape to National Service. I would get away, not only from Parkhead, but from girls, from bloody adolescence and from miserable me. I wasn't exactly joining the Foreign Legion, but for me, in April 1948, His Majesty's Royal Air Force felt like much the same thing. On the night before I left, my parents gave me a sending-off party at home with my mates. No girls. Dad got in some beers and I got drunk for the first time and was sick in the kitchen sink.

'Some people ur no' beer men,' my father had said as he watched.

'He's no' a man yet,' said my mother.

'Right enough,' said my father.

We Make Our Way

In the second quarter
We make our way
Come what may,
'But where?' we say
As we stumble through life's paper chase
Trying hard to maintain the pace,
Spreading out from childhood's race.
Proto-woman or not-quite man
Doing the very best we can
In our whirling, adolescent span.
We apply ourselves to the task in hand.
So much to learn, to understand
In education's foreign land:
Reports, certificates, diplomas, degrees
Hard to gain with appropriate ease.
It almost brings us to our knees.
But then comes graduation.
Capped and gowned, and duly crowned,
We can start to look around
For that fitting situation...
But careering madly from pillar to post
Travelling widely from coast to coast
For the sake of a salary boast
Is not what we thought.
Or imagined we ought
To be up and doing.
What have we bought?
Security's corset is not for us,
Nor a lifetime's routine truss,
The question now is what can we do
With whatever it is we have in view?
Why not make a completely fresh start
And what better place than in your heart?

CHAPTER FOUR

Finding Uniformity

There are no foreign lands. It is the traveller only who is foreign.

ROBERT LOUIS STEVENSON

THE ENIGMA OF LIVING is that everything has within it its opposite or shadow self, serving as a counterpoint to the face we put on to the world. The hidden self is there to balance the outward show but the actual self is a combination of both. It is an operation always in tandem and available because duality is a natural state. It is where reality co-exists with the imagination to present a composite, which is often accepted as the real front, since it is all we can physically see. A shadow is seen when a person walks ahead of the sun or moon, but an even greater shadow, metaphorically speaking, is cast when that same person walks ahead of himself and loses contact with his centre. Shadows always look younger than we do, because they are only in outline, they lack an interior. We are all more substantial than our shadows and deserve to be treated as the complicated bodies we are. We are our own production line and should only be concerned with what we might produce.

Now I had no choice about my outside self. It was to be in uniform. No sartorial bravado now, I was to throw off all previous identity and become a number. I was braced for the worst, and ready to be two-faced about it. Instead, I was pleasantly surprised by the service life I was introduced to in Lancashire, but I was no stranger to foreign parts. I had been out of Scotland before. To London in wartime and before that, as an infant, I had been carried on the steamer to Ireland, and went there many times as I grew up. Although it was another country, it was hardly foreign, as I was meeting more or less the same kind of people I had left behind in Glasgow. Aunts, uncles, cousins and friends that I had known for most of my life and welcomed me – family. But going to Padgate was a genuine foreign experience because that kind of England was completely new to me. Whether I liked it or not, I was suddenly being exposed to the rest of Britain, and I was the one who felt foreign.

On Monday 5 April 1948, I caught the train from the Central Station, Glasgow to the Royal Air Force and embarked on a new life in uniform. This journey was undertaken lightly, as are most life-changing excursions. I was sent off by my mates in a wave of laughter as if I were going on holiday, which indeed I felt I was, to that nearby land called England. It was a change certainly, but I didn't know that the two-year stint 'On His Majesty's Service' was to turn me upside down, shake out all my self-applied nonsense, and set me back on my two feet with all ten toes pointed to where I wanted to go. That was important enough, but it was two years away and not at all on my current horizon. This was *now*, and I had to admit, that while I was hesitant and unsure about how exactly to cope with all these new challenges, I was excited at the same time.

What a pity the Government decided to dispense with National Service for all young men between the ages of 18 and 20. It was exactly the cold shower needed during that age span. It offered an all expenses paid, all-round life experience that few could afford and threw them among their peers from all walks, now lined up on parade alongside them to march in step as best we could. The infant actor and erstwhile artist became a number overnight: 2359962. It is still in my brain 65 years later. I swelled to fit the Air Force blue but kept the Windsor knot in my tie. There are some things in life we never change.

Here I was, one adolescent, unsophisticated, apolitical Glaswegian going out into the wide world for the first time with no sense of where he really belonged in this new order of things. As I keep inferring, it is not what we do over the years, but how we live in the moment. This calls for an unreasonable optimism perhaps, but it's worth it, if we can drain from every experience all the good we can get, no matter how unlikely. Concentrate on what we can get from our own lives in any situation, but spread its effect as far as you can. In time, if it's any good at all, it can hide the sky. Even if we don't find our star and stumble along the way, ours is not to worry. Falling down is part of life, getting up is part of living.

I was in Northern England, yet it might have been North Wales, since every bed in my particular billet except mine was occupied by a Welsh-speaking Welshman. It was nothing more than a bureaucratic fluke, but all the same it meant that nation had to speak unto nation here and Scotland felt somewhat overwhelmed by sheer force of numbers. It was my first taste of genuine *foreign*. Apart from the brief flirtation with wartime Cockneys in London and soft-spoken Gaelic Highlanders in Perthshire, this was my first close encounter with another tongue. I was intrigued but mystified. It was also my initial exposure to the sheer power of nationality.

Among this enforced fellowship of boys striving to be men – a uniformed multiplicity of maleness on the rise – were people of my own age, fellow Celts, talking freely in a language unknown to me and proud to do so. The Welsh boys, from both North and South of the Principality (it wasn't even a country) were surprised that I didn't have the Gaelic. They told me I should be ashamed of myself not to be fully Scottish. I responded by telling them that I was Glaswegian first, and Scottish next. They couldn't understand that.

The military atmosphere of RAF Padgate was far removed from anything I had known in my 18 years. In that time, I had lived in a miner's cottage, a tenement room and kitchen, a Borders mansion house, a Highland estate and an earl's castle – now I found myself in a wooden Air Force barracks surrounded by Taffies who called me Jock. I refused to answer to the name and it soon was dropped. It was my first overt statement of identity and I felt proud that I had made a stand, but really it was a very minor victory.

Living for me at this stage meant finding my voice. And it turned out to be a tenor. I had been a boy soprano in the cathedral choir at one time and when the voice broke it stayed in the higher range, which was just right for Irish ballads, the only songs I knew as a boy. Quite unexpectedly, this store of folk material was to become the first stepping-stone in my National Service career. Sometimes, it's what you did yesterday that decides what happens tomorrow. I learned this when the billet found I could sing, and was a tenor to boot. To the Welsh, a tenor voice was a great prize. They taught me their Welsh songs, and I went through my Scots and Irish songs repertoire for them. It sounded alright in the darkness of the hut after lights out, especially as the corporal in charge of the new recruits was Irish. Even a corporal must feel homesick at times and these poignant melodies helped.

Even if it was only a roomful of young men, tired after a long day, lying in the dark listening to a softly sung folk song with each of the listeners deep in their own thoughts, it was still an audience, and I went out to them. Their listening silence was the only accompaniment I needed and I knew, even in that lullaby half-hour, as it came to be known, I had made a lot of friends. To quote Ralph Waldo Emerson – 'The only way to have a friend is to be one'. I did my best. What is friendship after all, but love in smaller print? It pays to give any good friendship its special emphasis, to try to see your friends in a bolder font, as it were. If they are real friends, they will feel for you in the same way. I found contact was made in the way my Welsh pals responded to the night songs. Unfortunately, these harmonic sessions after lights-out were often punctured by snores and ended in raucous laughter when a loud fart was heard, but occasionally there were some lovely moments. A few of the boys, good singers themselves, would often add their own Welsh humming harmonies from their beds in 'pyjama pianissimo', and when this happened there was real night magic in the air.

It was easy to take refuge in the regimental formality of service life. Orders were given and obeyed. That was it. No thinking was required. We were happily cocooned in our own world with no real responsibilities except to ensure that the shine was on our buttons and polish on our boots. It wasn't hard to understand why Lawrence of Arabia ran away to the Air Force to escape from his fame in his own day. It was easy to become anonymous in the ranks, but it wasn't always so for me. I discovered that I was an outsider by disposition and preference. My singular position in the billet didn't bother me at all. In fact, I quietly revelled in it. At any rate it helped me come to grips with this new life discipline.

We all looked the same in uniform, so it was easier for all of us to feel the same. Added to which, these 'uniforms' were all my own age, at the same stage, and similarly conscripted, but in my particular billet, with the single difference of language and dialect. I had no alternative but to listen. My Scottishness and their Welshness were historically twin-based and that meant something.

Anything with Celtic in it always caught my interest, even if my Celtic connection had a soft 'C'. This link in turn generated enthusiasm, which kindled a sort of passion, which encouraged a feeling that engendered a fuller sense of kinship, and so we hacked out a kind of common ground. Balance and proportion are everything if any effect is to be made, and this was what I found most difficult. Especially when they discussed rugby, about which, at the time, I knew nothing. They weren't at all interested in my kind of football, and a few of them hadn't even heard of Celtic.

The only thing that united us in sport were the broadcasts by the BBC on the Test Matches from Lords and Edgbaston. It was incredible to sit in the canteen eating lunch and hear John Arlott's lazy West Country drawl as he described the action at the wicket. Cricket was almost as foreign to me as Welsh, but I knew when to keep quiet, and even began to enjoy the rare quiet it brought to the day. Except when the West Indies were winning.

What I didn't notice then, or even give a thought to, was that there were no Jamaicans or Asians on the station. It was a totally all-white establishment. There were other Scots in other huts, as well as Irish and disparate English, like Geordies, Cornishmen and Cockneys, but no blacks. It was therefore quite incomplete in terms of racial identity, but that's how Britain was in the late '40s. Two decades on, it would be a different matter. Very little would be uniform then, and this may be the cause of the various warring strategies that arise in the world from day to day. The trouble with world governance is that it is almost impossible to bring about because each country of whatever size or influence is forever pulling on its own strings and each gets entangled as they are pulled in every direction. No wonder everything ends up in knots. Is true purity of existence possible?

Word of our unusual singing sessions soon got around and I was the talk of the NAAFI, but one result was that I was called to the Warrant Officer's room to explain the 'dormitory disturbances' as he called them. The WO was a stuffy, middle-aged man from the Midlands. I explained that the sessions had happened spontaneously because the Welsh boys were musical and I merely obliged as requested. He still regarded it as a breach of billet discipline and asked why the corporal in charge didn't stop it.

'He likes it, Sir.'

'Well, I don't. I'll have to report it to the CO.'

That's when I got a big surprise.

I had been previously given an interview for a commission and this meant the possibility of actually flying, but when I went up before the Group Captain about the singing, I was told I had been turned down for Officer Training due to my weak left eye. This didn't completely distress me, but what did was the added comment on my 'lack of educational background'. This really hurt. I was minus that one piece of paper that would confirm I'd had a secondary education. Why hadn't I stayed on at St Mungo's? It was the first shock to my intellectual self-esteem, and I felt it. There was no mention at all about the night singing.

I was packed off to RAF Cardington, near Hereford. The town boasted a fine cathedral, but Hereford United somehow didn't have the same ring as Glasgow Celtic. I attended the local ground on the first Saturday but I couldn't get the buzz from it that I got every time at Celtic Park. I tried to adjust but could find no other stimulus to offset the total boredom of the accounts course. I missed my Welsh songsters and my Glasgow office job had already shown me that administration was not what I ever wanted to do. On a whim, I went to my Flight Commander and asked to be posted overseas.

'Any preferences?' he asked.

'China.'

'Pass your accounts course and we will see what can be done.'

'Oh.'

I was deflated again – accounts? Not my thing at all. The best way to deal with any disappointment is to get some good out of it. If I needed that course, I would bloody well get it. Determination will help any ambition and there is no greater incentive than self-determination. And a bit of indignation helps. I applied myself to the ledgers by day and at night I enjoyed the social hour at the NAAFI, where I swallowed my distaste for beer and enjoyed the singsongs – but not in Welsh. These singing occasions led to my doing some tenor solos, standing on a table. This got to the ear of my CO and once again I was standing to attention in front of him, but I was not on the carpet for ruining NAAFI furniture. He had other ideas.

'Stand easy, aircraftsman,' he said kindly. 'In view of your – err – performing propensities, I think it might be better if we transferred you from Accounts to Entertainments.'

'Yes, Sir.' I could have cheered.

'I understand you put in a request for a posting abroad?'

'Yes, Sir.'

'That could also be arranged, but not to China, I'm afraid.'

'No, Sir?'

'No. But given your entertainment qualifications, we could send you immediately to Germany.'

'Germany?'

'To help maintain the Berlin Airlift. And, if you go in – what shall we say? – your theatrical capacity, we needn't worry unduly about accounts qualifications, need we?'

'No, Sir.' I couldn't help smiling.

'And if I were you, I would go for that Forces Prelim paper if you get the chance. It might come in handy. That will be all, aircraftsman. *Viel Glück*.'

'Sir?'

'It's "Good Luck" in German.'

'Thank you, Sir.'

Germany was a name I had grown up with, but for me it was the name of a menace, an enemy, a dark Nazi arm that aimed to kill, that dropped bombs on civilians and killed Jews. But it was also the country that produced Martin Luther, who started all the religious bother, the Bach family, Beethoven, Karl Marx and Bertolt Brecht, not to mention Marlene Dietrich. It couldn't be all bad. It was a part of the European continent, a piece of territory on the earth like our little bit of it across the Channel. Its citizens were just people, blood and bone people like us, more or less. It was only that they were unlucky to land up with Hitler and his gang at the wrong time. They spoke a different language, not a different dialect.

At least, that was my thinking as I flew in a plane for the first time. A shaky old Lancaster transport, extremely uncomfortable, with bench seats for about a dozen other ranks and not a parachute between us. We landed with some relief, and a bump or two, in Hanover airport. It was a weird sight that greeted us. Hanover seemed like a tented village set in a quarry. It was not unlike London as I remembered it, except that it wasn't red. It was black and white and every shade of grey. Streets were narrow corridors cleared of rubble, with the ruins of buildings lowering behind like stone sentinels. It was eerie. Yet it was not frightening, because life went on, in and around the debris. People had survived this?

I was reminded of something the American playwright William Saroyan had written:

> In the time of your life, live... Seek goodness everywhere, and when it is found, bring it out of its hiding place and let it be free and unashamed.

This was not the easiest thing to do in post-war Germany. This prideful country did not take defeat easily, but it saw that it had only itself to blame for giving their little Führer a free rein. However, it was hurting more from the previous war's end in 1918 than the recent armistice in 1945. The Treaty of Versailles, spurred on by the French, not only brought the old Germany down but pushed its face in the mud and then trod on it. There was no grace in the peace. The merciless victors of that first Great War saw no further than their own revenge. Germany was further punished by the rise of the Nazis and the outbreak of the Second World War in 1939. Hitler was accepted only because he promised to restore national pride.

By 1945, here she was, wasted yet again with tents for shops in the blitzed town centres and queues on every corner for fresh water. Yet the first building to be rebuilt in Hanover, as far as I could see at the end of 1948, was Der Konzertsaal, the town concert hall. In Glasgow it would have been the pub, in Wales, the chapel, in England the Town Council Offices, but it was the Concert Hall in Hanover and it was already open and offering music to the citizens. This was the first of the two great seminal events that Germany afforded a certain ACI in uniform and I grasped the first with both hands – or rather, both ears.

I had never been to a concert of classical music in my life. The only knowledge I had of it was my memory of the Earl of Cluny's heavy 78 rpm gramophone records. This was the chance to hear it live. And here I was, sitting in the front row, legs spread out wide, my cap in the epaulette on my shoulder, waiting for the concert to begin. As far as I could see I was the only serviceman there. There were officers up in the box to my right, but I couldn't see them properly. I did notice, though, that the stalls behind me were packed with civilians. A dull mass they made in old clothes and mufflers, but they could have lit the hall from the collective sparkle in their eyes. They obviously loved their music.

This was shown as they rose as one to greet the conductor. He was a tall, slim, bald man with a solemn face who went on to the podium, gave a cursory bow, then, turning to the orchestra, raised his baton. This was Maestro Wilhelm Furtwängler, possibly one of the finest conductors in the world at that time, and only recently cleared by the de-nazification court to resume his musical career. Now I watched closely as he was about to conduct a concert, which I thought, in my innocence, was entirely for my benefit.

What happened over the next two hours was a revelation to me. It was not only my first concert, but my first hearing of Wagner's overture to 'Tristan und Isolde' and my introduction to Beethoven's Symphony No 6, the 'Pastoral'. It was also my first acquaintance with the world-class talent of Furtwängler and to the whole evidence of oneness he drew from the orchestra. No posh dinner jackets and bow ties – this was wardrobe as found, but it was music from the heavens. All I saw of the famous conductor, of course, was the back of his head, but what I heard him coax out of the orchestra was from another sphere. I was truly spellbound and was converted for life to classical music from those first few bars.

I wasn't aware until then that music heard in live performance could have such power or that it could play on the senses in such a way. And on all parts of the body. My chest was tight, my throat dry and my heart was pounding. It was a complete, sedentary workout. All it needed was for my toes to curl and the hair to rise on the back of my neck. I had to concentrate, but it was well worth it.

There is a curative element in music, and it is a medicine that can only be good for us. My first taste of it was undoubtedly beneficial, although the diminished chords in the 'Tristan' played havoc with my entire nervous system. I was thoroughly engaged and braced, all senses geared, for the Beethoven. I wasn't disappointed. This was a far cry from the Earl of Cluny's 78rpm records. It was the real thing, German music by German musicians for a German audience in a German hall. It could not fail. Beethoven's conversation with trees and flowers, blackbirds and cuckoos in the forest outside Vienna was there in every inspired note. It got the standing ovation it deserved and no one stood taller than this virgin listener who had just been baptised in the holy waters of Beethhoven.

Probably not many in that audience had eaten properly that day, or were going home to a cosy bed, but they knew they had all shared in a feast of artistic effort and found that it can help one to live a little easier, whatever the circumstances. Good art of any kind can make us feel good and if we feel good, it can at least help us to cope. You can't eat a symphony or an opera, but both can make us forget what else we can't do, or can't have – or the particular condition we're in, if it's not all that comfortable. Good music well played in concert does exactly the same thing. Art works, that's what we have to remember. It affects us by what it does to our senses, even if it is only for the moment, but it has a capacity to affect that is timeless.

It is called catharsis, but I didn't know that then. What I did know was that I had heard something beautiful and wonderful and echoes of it still sounded in my head as I walked back to my quarters. The whole event's effect kept me awake in my bunk and there was no folk lullaby to lull me to sleep this time, only the memory of unforgettable chords. What I couldn't get over was the sheer power of the evening's music and the way it cut me off from time, leaving me free to live in the golden moment of artistic impact when we can't do anything but surrender to it. It was hard to get up the next morning and keep my mind on figures and facts and on arranging auditions for would-be singers and comedians on RAF stations within our area. I was still suffering from the after-effects of my first love session with an orchestra.

Post-war Germany opened up the whole, wide world to me. I was to take enormous strides forward in the size nine boots issued. I did so because I had the feeling that this might be my last chance to find the particular route that would take me to whatever. It was only a hunch, but I was learning to trust this instinct. This was why I acted on my old CO's advice and enrolled in a Forces Education Course that would gain me University Entrance if I ever needed it. I got down to serious study right away. This did not make me the most efficient Accounts Clerk or temporary Entertainments Assistant, but it made me feel a little better about being Aircraftsman First Class. I was encouraged by a remark made at the first session by the Flying Officer in charge of the Education programme,

'If you try 100 per cent you can't fail 100 per cent.'

I took up every outlet of learning available to me. I was conscious of making up for lost time, of hurrying because I knew I had wasted too much time already. To know how to properly manage time is the first step towards learning anything. I was exhilarated at being given a second chance. I was being taught the importance of rigour. Courses were gobbled up as they came along and I was flying. I learned to ski, took horse-riding lessons and completed a leadership course in Celle, another town, not far away.

There was a young English priest there, Father Basset, who gave me a prayer book with the written inscription, '"What is Truth?" said Pilate.' Father Basset thought that was something an erstwhile actor might ponder. The young priest also gave me a good bit of advice:

'Before you go anywhere in life,' he said, 'pack well. By that I mean, not shirts and socks, but look carefully into yourself. You'll find everything you need on the journey there.'

It was something I confess I didn't always act on, but I never forgot its good sense – or the man who said it.

Anything and everything was grist to my self-improvement mill and I sang as I cruised along as very small part of an entertainment programme that encouraged personnel to entertain themselves. On my desk now, instead of sheaves of accounts, there were lists of would-be serviceman who wanted to audition. I couldn't have been happier. All were other ranks, no officers ever applied. They must have regarded themselves as strictly audience material. Be that as it may, I made my way from NAAFI to clubhouse to church hall and tented auditorium, listening, talking and singing, having the time of my life with my kind of people.

I didn't know that another storm was blowing up on the horizon and was gradually heading my way. Her name was Hilburga. She could only be German but to me, she was a petite Ingrid Bergman. She spoke English and was employed by the Air Force base as a part-time translator. I had met her in the Malcolm Club, Cologne, when I helped organise a local choir to sing some German carols in the club at Christmas. The CO thought it would help relations between the Armed Forces and the community but, on the night, we reckoned without the demon drink.

Some soldiers – Scots, I'm sorry to say – objected to the sound of German voices in a British club and started to shout from the back and generally cause a nuisance. They started singing their own tuneless, mock version of 'Deutschland, Deutschland über Alles' and the men in the German choir naturally retorted with a very loud real version; mayhem resulted. The two groups moved menacingly towards each other. In no time, bottles were flying. I dived under the nearest table and found that I had company. It was Hilburga, in a woollen hat and raincoat on over her concert dress. She immediately threw her arms around me.

'John, it is not good,' she cried as another crash was heard. Instinctively, I put my arms around her and it felt *very* good. 'Come on, let's get out of here.'

With her coat over both of us we somehow forced our way through the melee and got out to the front door.

'Sorry about all that,' I said.

'It's not your blame,' she said in that sexy accent. 'Your soldiers not like our music.'

'They're not my soldiers,' I told her.

We stood looking at each other for a moment with the battle still going on behind the front door. A jeep carrying Military Police screeched to a halt in front of us. I pulled her aside as they rushed past us and into the club. When they had gone in, I was still holding her closely. She looked up at me.

'*Gehen mir zu meinem Haus?*'

'Sorry?'

'You will walk me to my house?'

'Ja, I will,' I said in a voice that I didn't think was mine.

When I first saw the framed photograph of her husband in the bedroom I was surprised at how young he looked in his naval uniform.

'He die under sea,' whispered Hilburga from behind me. 'Under sea' could only mean submarines – U-boats.

'Were you married long?' I asked, still looking at the photograph.

'Two weeks.'

I turned quickly away. I couldn't think what to say.

'He was called Hans,' she went on, and started to undress.

I could only stare as she continued to disrobe without the least embarrassment.

'You will remove your dress?' she said with a smile.

'Of course.'

What followed could only be described as a masterclass in the art of lovemaking by a young widow who was a mistress in every sense of the word, introducing its delights in a manner appropriate to a partner whom she instinctively knew was effectively innocent. She had decided to make love, which is a lot different to the usual male approach to initiating sexual intercourse. In her woman's way, she had guessed my virginity and was now showing me so very gently and beautifully what the love-act at its best should be. For her, it was a shared event between two beings, not a rowdy invasion by one. She illustrated this by holding her two clenched fists pressed hard against each other.

'*Nein*,' she said. Then joined her palms as if in prayer, '*Ja*,' she whispered, pressing only the index fingers together. '*Ein!*' she added. '*Keine Eile und Hektik. Milde und leise. Sanft.*'

I had about four words of German but I got her meaning... 'Soft, gentle and sweet.' And thus, I went with her, slowly, step by step, on a joint odyssey of the body that was as momentous to me as the Wagner and Beethoven had been in the Konzertsaal. Afterwards, she lay back smiling, and whispered something like '*Ich haben genug.*'

It sounded like Bach to me. The ecstasy that music had given me artistically had now been replicated physically and lifted me to the same heights. It was culture and coitus combined and it was an irresistible combination for any 19-year-old at the height of his sexual powers. This was no Edinburgh fiasco but a virtual opera of sensation. I couldn't get the musical analogy out of my mind because I had just learned that sex *is* music, playing on the same senses that respond to sound, which is why music, good music, is love and must be received as such.

I had lost my virginity to a daughter of the Herrenvolk, who triumphantly seduced me and took time to do so. I had finally gained my manhood and sang her a rugby song in Welsh in gratitude. It was nearly dawn when I came out into the outside landing and gave a Hitler salute to a neighbour who peeked through her curtain. I was drunk with sexual satiation, something I had never known before. I was high, because my whole being had been lifted up on to a new plane. But I had little time to enjoy my new state. I was arrested in the street by RAF Regiment Police for drunken behaviour. Although I wasn't drunk, I must have seemed so and that was enough for police minds. I was put in *jankers* for the day, which meant I was effectively behind bars.

I might have paid dearly for my love night, but for the fact that my demobilisation papers had come through the previous day and, on the intervention of my CO, who guessed that it was a case of unpremeditated AWOL, which to me meant Absence with Outstanding Love. I was hurriedly bundled onto an aeroplane bound for RAF Stanmore without a chance to see Hilburga again. I was really sorry about that. This charming girl, a young widow who had so little material comforts in her home, had orchestrated my first real sexual encounter with all the control, finesse and discipline of a Furtwängler. On the plane I couldn't get her out of my mind. Hilburga was the wife of a U-boat commander lost at sea, yet she behaved with me like a young girl in love for the first time.

Furtwängler no doubt went on to his next musical engagement not knowing the havoc he had caused in one young man's musical awareness. I still had the vision of Hilburga in her patched skirt and woollen cardigan hiding a form that deserved the finest of dresses. I would have loved to see her again, but in another way I didn't want to. I wanted nothing to spoil a special memory. Our coming together was no more than a trivial encounter in the greater scheme of things, I knew that, but for me all previous standards were shaken. Even what was right or wrong seemed immaterial. I had given to her because she had given so freely to me. It had happened mutually, and that's what love must be, total mutuality. Hilburga had never said she loved me, but I was convinced that for one wonderful moment she did. I certainly did in that same moment.

Germany had never invaded Britain in the war, but it had invaded me. First, in re-educating me, then allowing me to discover music, and lastly, to crown it all, given me my first real sexual encounter. These events were more than life-changing, they were life-enhancing and they were to return me now to Glasgow and Civvy Street as an unashamed man. Innocence is armour, if we know how to wear it, but I had just outgrown it. It was time to cast it off.

I needed now to rely on a new *savoir-faire* or, at best, a studied insouciance, to carry me forward. It was as if I had gone to that foreign country for the sole purpose of being seduced, first by music then by a beautiful female, so that both happenings could effect a complete reordering of my whole sense of being.

Third Interval

The New Generation

We are not the supine hostages to history.
We belong in the present, guardians of the mystery
That lies behind the curtain of tomorrow.
The brimming cup of happiness,
The leaden draught of sorrow,
Whichever it may be,
We will drink it down.
Fortune's a thief, and Fame is a clown.
If you will scale the mountain peak
Then let that triumph for you speak,
Or, should you sink into the abyss,
Be of good heart, and think of this:
You 'might-have-been', but instead,
You are!
You can still reach up
And touch that star.

CHAPTER FIVE

A Work in Progress

Youth is not a time of life – it is a state of mind… a temperamental predominance of courage over timidity, of the appetite of adventure over a life of ease.

SAMUEL ULLMAN

A CONTEMPORARY POET and friend of mine, Angus Reid, said in a poem of his, 'All I am is what I'm doing right now.' With great respect to Angus, I think what he is doing is within his being. Being is all and constant. We may be continually obsessed by what we do, and even identified by it. 'What does he do?' is a loaded question in every sense. John Ford's invention of the conveyor belt system of car manufacture virtually created the American city of Detroit, but it reduced his work-force to little more than robots forced to forego their humanity for the sake of increased efficiency. Detroit is currently in decline as a result, because Ford forgot that people are greater than even the most sophisticated of systems, and machines will rot and rust before the spirit dies in man. Human beings are not machine parts, they are individual lives and therefore irreplaceable.

The Internet exerts the same Fordian tyranny today by means of computers, mobile phones, laptops, iTablets, Kindle books and all the other handheld gadgetry of the technical age which, in my opinion, combine to lessen the direct control of our own lives, and therefore detract from any full sense of being. Not that the young of today care much about that. They are the new dictators, the post-adolescent emperors of the age, mobile sceptres in hand, giving voice to their own generation. They Twitter and tweet and blog and post in the imperious manner that tells us they are in charge of themselves; they are the technicians of the techno-age who abide by the rules of their God, the Internet, a deity their peers so recently invented. The contemporary mania for libertine and illiterate mass communication within the social media threatens to kill the considered word, whether written or spoken, and its future seems to be in the hands of our children. The new young thrive on the hyper-availability of trivial matter and have no need whatsoever of encouragement or incentive, pen and paper, fresh air and exercise or anyone older than 20.

The streets of any city in the world are now full of people staring at their hands instead of looking where they are going. Do they feel the wind in their hair or the rain on the faces? They are losing so much in actual life experience, not to mention sleep, in order to gain such little social benefit by being constantly up-to-date with everything and everybody. If we go on like this, we are in great danger of losing one of the main elements of human attractiveness – mystery.

No one was more aware of this than the former Aircraftsman First Class/Clerk/Entertainer, now returned to civilian life as a practised, off-the-cuff tenor, a hardly-begun actor and an unfinished art student. I didn't know how and where to make a re-start. The big difference was that the plastic, unanchored mentality of my adolescence had been moulded into something firmer by the Teutonic experience. I was in fact remade in Germany and grateful for it. This was not only the sexual coming of age, but an all-round burgeoning of aesthetic susceptibility and response. The truth was I had emerged from the little matchbox that was my East End, pre-Air Force self and developed enough to fill a shoebox once I donned a uniform. But then the hatbox that was Germany opened up and put the lid on me. The twin musical and sexual eruptions had blown that lid sky high and left me hanging in space, but somehow with one foot still touching the ground.

I had not yet learned to put my future behind me, and let it push me forward. This is the gift of the mature and demands a rigorous intellectual effort that was certainly not mine at the time. I had yet to learn how to exist in the present, to live off the air I breathed, especially the smoky air of dear old Glasgow. Certainly I had piled up a few more memories, but now I was returning to my own city, out of uniform, free at least of the similar cordon my city had put round me pre-RAF. I was no longer chained to all those inchoate desires that had so plagued my earlier adolescent years. I was now the National Service version of myself, but still too young to know what to do with it. I had to stop acting my age and have the courage to be it.

In April 1950, I was 20 years old, but in comparison with the same generation today, I was dumb and static. All I could say about myself was that I had black hair, hazel eyes, was 5 foot 11 inches in height and weighed 11 stone. At least, that was what was said in my RAF passbook, and it was all that could be said about my physique. It didn't say anything about my state of mind. I thought a 'change of life' was something that happened to women of a certain age, but I was definitely feeling a stranger to myself. I felt like a tulip – pale at the tip with the mere thought of making a place for myself in the world, blushing pink at the temerity of even thinking that I might just make it wherever I aimed, and deep purple all over when it dawned on me what effort would be required. But big decisions were looming.

The last thing I wanted was a job – another desk, a routine occupation that I would attend every day until my old age pension. I couldn't do that. I was a natural 'freelance' but the only question was, where would I point it? We are told that at all times we must be doing, but what could I do with any real confidence? I could talk, sing, draw, but I was still uncertain which was my true vocation: art or acting? I wasn't even sure about being. I didn't know whether to apply to my heart or my brain for the answer. I looked inside myself, deeply, and couldn't see a thing. Natural intuition was at war with still-limited experience, no matter my various attempts at sophistication, and both states applied to education as reference. My education was still a work in progress, admittedly now at a more reasonable level, but it was the same old tug of war between the subjective feeling and the objective assessment of what was required to give me some kind of confidence in searching for a purpose. It was an ongoing battle. I was fighting with myself and in that kind of battle, nobody wins. All I wanted was the certainty of vocation, but there is no certainty in any life and without vocational trust, no artistic way is tenable.

From the earliest of times, the better artists seemed to know exactly who they were and where they were. In a book found in his library, Holbein wrote in Latin, 'I am Johannes Holbein, whom it is easier to denigrate than to emulate.' I admire that kind of honesty. It brooks no dispute. Perhaps I ought to have lived in the mid-to-late 18th-century Age of Enlightenment, when introspection was all the fashion and the vogue was to be fascinated by oneself. From the mid-18th century to the first decade of the

19th, philosophers investigated the question of identity and writers like Burns, Wordsworth and Rousseau tried their best to keep up with them. The latter admitted in his *Confessions*: 'Myself alone! I know the feelings of my heart, and I know men. I am not made like any of those I have seen.' Burns, too, wrote, 'To know myself has been my constant study – I weighed myself alone.' And Wordsworth would write *The Prelude, or Growth of a Poet's Mind*.

It was a case of self-obsession with these fine writers, the need to know themselves better so as to use that self in the service of their literary aims. No matter what field, the artist of any kind is driven by the same self-created purpose, which is to render, in explicit form, the stimulation of his creative imagination and share it with others as a visual or aural experience. To do so, he or she draws on the unlimited bank balance of his or her mind, and in return the best fee they can get is lay appreciation. I do not for a moment suggest that I'm peer with such talents, but I do know, and I guessed then, that I was all artist and it had to come out one way or another before I could get down to working on it. I had to earn my living.

Ironically, the first thing discussed in any artistic project is the money, but the artist only needs the money so that he can go on being an artist. Only among themselves will freelance artists agree that they would do what they do for nothing, for the pleasure in doing. There is no greater reward than satisfaction in a job well done. Pride in doing is not vanity, but the self-reward for the effort involved. False pride is a mask that the uncertain wear to boost their own inadequacy. The secret is to know our own worth honestly, according to our own standards and not by anybody else's. Sadly, in all artistic work it's that 'anybody' who makes all the decisions. The seller and the buyer, not the maker, rule today. The curator often has a greater say in art matters than the artist. Those who can, do, those who can't, talk about it.

I found that there were many such people on my return to Glasgow. They were full of wise saws but they did not cut much ice with me. I realised that freedom of thought and action was worth a lot more than stability and a regular income. I leaned naturally to the kind of work where the ego is central to the activity, but I knew that it was the stomach that needed the money. However, I guessed, too that to think of working in any artistic profession is to court anarchy. It's dangerous, but it's an exciting, thrilling danger. What I didn't realise was that I was searching for a passion. I needed an outlet that utilised my innermost feelings, deep down in the engine room. Only football did that for me at this time, and in a much lesser way still does.

My young brother Jim was the footballer in the family and was making a very good living at it. I did try at one stage to be a goalkeeper. After all, both Albert Camus and Arthur Conan Doyle played in goal for football clubs at one time, so I had worthy examples to follow. But it never excited me the way performing did, or playing with ideas on canvas or paper. However, I was still on the lookout for the particular means of expression that might be mine. So far, things had just happened to me without my seeming to do anything about it. It was like walking along a corridor with doors opening as I passed by. I just went along with things and when any door closed on me, another invariably opened. And that's how theatre came into my life.

Let's face it; if we want to be noticed, we have to take notice. If we want to be wanted, it helps to know first what is wanted, and that is where I felt particularly inadequate. I had so little practical experience of either art or theatre. I could easily have returned to Art School or gone back to the Park Theatre, which had now become the Festival Theatre in Pitlochry, Perthshire. It was then in a marquee tent, but I had no wish to go under canvas. How could I break clear of this cleft stick? I did so by enrolling at university.

Flaunting my RAF credentials, I matriculated at Glasgow to do English. I got a little card with my name in Latin. Somehow 'Johannes' seemed more official, even ancient. Which was appropriate, as my university was approaching its 500th birthday and I was a year away from coming of age. The Latin tag also reminded of my first supposed vocation at 12, when the teachers and priests in their wisdom thought I should become a Marist. I was all for it at the time because it meant getting out of polluted Parkhead for an education at a boarding school near Dumfries. I liked the idea of a large library, swimming pool, cricket pitch, football pitch and tennis courts all being available, but none of them was, to my mind, reason enough for entering the church.

I never became a priest in the end, because my mother was suddenly convinced, quite correctly, that it was not right for me. My father didn't say much, other than I should think myself lucky that I had the kind of Continental experience that the toffs used to send their sons off to, usually accompanied by a tutor. They called it the Grand Tour and Dad quietly pointed out that I had had mine, with tutors in all fields, he gathered, but I couldn't live indefinitely 'on the hoose', which meant on his wages. I had to start looking around for a way to earn my keep. I couldn't go back to my mother's kitchen table. But where to start? I had many conversations on this topic that summer – with cousin Margaret in Baillieston, with Canon Rooney of St Bridget's, also in Baillieston, who urged me to go back to Art School, with best pal, Bill Hutcheson, who was now a trainee manager at Marks and Spencer's. I had written his application for him. When I wrote on my own behalf and got an interview in town, I was turned down. My indifference must have shown. The only person I had no real conversation with was my fiancée. Was I ducking some issue there? We sat silent in the cinema or walked in the park talking about other people. She was no fool, she thought I was just 'at a stage' and would come through it.

If we have a real vocation, for anything, we have no doubts. It never feels like work, we just have to do it. We learn to use all the equipment we've got – the inside motor and the outside wheel – so that we can drive ourselves as hard as we like along the route we take because we feel safe on the road. That was the feeling I wanted, what I was searching for. It was then that life, or Providence (or the Glasgow Education Department), came to the rescue up with a trump card in the form of the new College of Drama, which was due to open later that year as part of the Royal Scottish Academy of Music at the Athenaeum in St George's Place.

I only found out about it when I went there to enquire about singing lessons, to have my tenor voice properly trained. This was yet another option, and it was while enquiring about it that I found out about the Drama College. Out at once went all thoughts of singing lessons, and I asked if I could combine drama training with university. They said that Poetics and the History of Dramatic Representation were already in the curriculum, linked to lectures at Gilmorehill. Even better. I had wasted a whole summer already and I couldn't wait to get started. How do I get in? 'You have to audition,' I was told. So I prepared Hamlet's 'Advice to the Players' as it was the only prose piece of any length that would conform to their request for something from Shakespeare. The only reaction I got from the Director sitting in the auditorium was: 'What's wrong with your voice? Do you have a cold?'

It was to be the first of many comments on my voice, good and bad, throughout my career. Nevertheless, because I was male – men were scarce at drama school auditions – and no doubt owing something to my previous acting experience, I got in. I couldn't wait to tell my parents. I was now officially set to begin proper training for a life on the stage. My father wasn't too pleased: 'Paint your face, and talk like a lassie,' he said.

My mother's reaction was more encouraging.

'Leave him, Tom. It's just the daft kinna joab that'll suit him.'

How right she was.

And so, on a September morning, I was there on the doorstep of the new Drama College in St George's Place, as it was then called, with 19 other drama hopefuls, all standing at the door only to find our way barred by a little man in a black bowler hat and wing collar holding up a large placard which read:

DO NOT ENTER HERE.
THEATRE IS A PLACE OF SIN.
DO NOT YIELD TO THE DEVIL.
TURN AWAY FROM TEMPTATION.

Oddly enough, I was quite touched by this display. How brave of a wee Glasgow gentleman to scroll his beliefs in large letters for all to see, to stand there on the pavement with his wife beside him in support, her handbag in hand before her, risking the jeers and laughter of passers-by as well as the total apathy of the students she and her husband were attempting to deter. How wonderful that he should have the enthusiasm to prepare such a banner in the first place, then to proudly hold it up for all to see. There might have been an element of fanaticism in his evangelical zeal, but there was obvious sincerity as well, and that has to be admired.

Conviction like this is rare. I rather envied him for it. The loyalty of the wife, too, standing beside him, was touching. What they didn't realise, however, that it was in answer to my own devils that I was there in the first place. I was desperate to enter because I wanted to exorcise them by using them theatrically. The possibility of sin was something I hadn't thought of, but I didn't mind the temptation. Giving him a quick pat on the shoulder, I ducked under the banner and ran up the steps and through the door to my future.

What I knew in my life from this moment on and for the next three years can only be described as elation. Any journey is happy when we think we know where we're going. All doubts disappeared and I plunged into new waters with all the relish of the convert. It was indeed almost a religious fervour in beginning yet another era in my life. I couldn't get up early enough each day. I was in love again, with my studies and with everyone concerned. All of a sudden, I had a genuine purpose. Mine was an acting, singing, dancing, miming, fencing existence with novelties added like the Alexander Technique and Dalcroze Eurhythmics. Everything about my drama training interested and intrigued me. I went boldly in search of Thespis and the aboriginal theatrical tradition that began with Aristotle, and here I was, drinking it all in behind the stone walls of Glasgow's new College of Dramatic Art.

It was almost too much, but in many ways, it wasn't enough. My appetite for learning was fully wetted, although learning to speak English properly was an unexpected hurdle. For instance, I had to learn that 'whitturyeuptythen?' sounded better as 'How are you doing?' and 'No bother' was no longer 'naeborra'. It was hard to drop the habits of a lifetime, but it was to be worth it, as Glaswegian is hardly the accepted voice of classical theatre. The first off-stage English words I ever uttered were in response to an old pal at Parkhead Cross who asked me, 'Whit time's it?'

'Twen-ty-min-utes-to-nine,' I replied, carefully enunciating every syllable.

He looked at me oddly. 'Whit's up wi' you?'

'I'm speaking English.'

'Oh, aye. Whit fur?'

'I am going to be an ak-tor.' I said in my best adjudicator manner. My pal was not impressed.

'Ye'r aff yer heid.'

This was the general reaction. Parkhead people thought I was mad. Not for the last time, but I was oblivious to every catcall. I *knew* I was on my way. I even tried my new accent at home, much to my mother's amusement. Lingua frankly, she was a little uncertain about this metamorphosis, but the overnight aesthete kept better hours than her teenage ne'er-do-well – and she was glad to get her kitchen table back.

The East End retreated as the West End gradually took over, leaving only the non-perishable strand that tied me to Celtic Football Club, although the boys' gate was now exchanged for the enclosure opposite the main stand. The little East End scruff was still in the young theatrical man, and whatever fancy dress I now chose to wear, there was always a green and white jersey underneath. That particular love affair was for life.

On the other hand, my love affair with my fiancée was on less firm ground. We were still engaged, but now met only on weekends for that walk in the park or a trip into town for a film, then back to my house or hers for a meal. It was pleasant enough, but it was all rather formal and more social than sexy. A quick peck at the end of the night lasted both of us for the week. Our relationship seemed to rely more on duty and obligation than any feelings of passionate love. We were recognised as a couple, but while I was still was a student on a grant, I rather let things lie. Sometimes the best action is no action. However, inaction is only laziness. I was lazy in this particular matter. Marriage was never discussed.

All my energies were given over to speaking in my elementary English voice as Algernon in Oscar Wilde's *The Importance of Being Earnest,* and being very earnest indeed about it in the Athenaeum Theatre, before an audience of relations and friends. Although none of mine was there. I wasn't ready for that kind of scrutiny yet. I really enjoyed prancing about being English and I gradually moved up the pecking order until I was playing 'Everyman' in the medieval mystery play before a large audience of university students doing English. This was my first real 'swim' in theatrical waters and I took to it like a duck.

To make some extra money, I appeared with other drama students as an extra at the Citizens Theatre in the Gorbals. I loved the chance it gave us all to see some real acting. One production there, however, towards the end of my first year at the college, had unexpected repercussions – for me, at any rate. It was *King Lear* starring George Colouris, the Hollywood actor who had worked with Orson Welles. One of the students with us in the crowd dressing room was fellow student John Carlin. He had been a helper that morning at auditions for the new second intake at the College, and was raving about the beauty that had attended and sailed through, but he couldn't remember her name.

Everybody shouted out suggestions, mostly ribald, like 'Greta Garbo' and 'Shirley Temple'. For no reason, I took up a greasepaint stick from my tray and carefully wrote the name, 'Sheila Cowan' on my mirror space.

I asked John if that was the name.

'My God,' said John, 'I think it was. How did you know that?'

'I don't know. It just came into my head.'

'Come on. Who are you kidding? You must have seen the audition list.'

'I'm telling you, I've no idea who she is. I just wrote a name, that's all.'

'Amazing,' said my fellow extra, wryly. 'Magic moments, right enough.'

The rest of the room made the same kind of bantering comment, calling out absurd female names before getting on with the business of getting ready for the night's show, but I still sat staring at the name.

'Sheila Cowan? Who's she? What the hell made me do that?'

I tried to rub out the name but I just made a mess on the mirror.

What I didn't mention to my dressing-room colleagues was that it might have been my feyness – the gift of glimpsing the future in often inexplicable flashes. It was an intuitive faculty. My mother and my grandmother had the same foresight, except that my mother didn't think it a gift. 'You see things ye don't need to see,' she said.

It is a cognitive foresight, called 'fey' in Irish, and is usually a prerogative of the female, but I had it, and it was to make itself known at several points in my life, sometimes very disconcertingly. Precognition of any kind is not to be taken lightly. It is often Nature's warning sign, a signal out of nowhere, a call for action it might be dangerous to ignore. Why some have it and others don't is a matter of metabolism, or the result of a store of family genes going back over centuries. Whatever it is, or however gained, and from what source, it is knowledge and it is intended to be used by the seer.

Primary sight is often confused by having too many things in the lens at the same time, but precognition sees into our future by drawing from ancestral experience, which is why it's stored in families. I know there were things I knew intuitively about people, complete strangers that I had no wish to know and I had no idea why I knew it. I therefore put down this writing of a strange name on a dressing room mirror as just another one of those things and put it out of my mind. Once I was on stage with the others, I never gave the incident another thought. Until the first morning of the new term at Drama College.

At the start of a new session of 1952–53, our Director, Colin Chandler, took the opportunity to take a register of every student present, as it was the first time that the full three course years had been assembled. Everybody cheered. I paid only perfunctory attention until suddenly I heard the name 'Sheila Cowan' being called and my head jerked up. I was all attention now. But I couldn't see who had responded, only because the voice had come from a blonde girl sitting directly in front of me. I couldn't resist tapping her on the shoulder. She turned round – and smiled – wow! I was suddenly aware that I was looking at an extraordinarily attractive young girl still in her teens. She quickly turned away again, and I sat stupefied and could only watch as she rose to leave with the other girls.

I waited at the front door and when she came out, I waylaid her telling her I had written her name on a mirror. She wasn't impressed and kept walking. I chased after, still talking, until it started to rain real Glasgow rain and I pulled her into the nearest café for shelter. After some serious persuasion over the coffees I took her down to the Citz, as we called it, to see for herself, but the cleaners had erased the name completely. Nevertheless, for some reason Sheila believed me, or at least, said she did. Rather sheepishly we took the next tram back to the City Centre and left her at her hostel door in St Vincent Street.

I didn't sleep very well that night. I couldn't get her face out of my mind. Nor the sound of her voice when she said, 'Okay, I believe you.' From that moment I had a strong hunch that complications were about to arise and I felt I could do nothing about it. I was engaged to be married to a girl I knew and loved – or thought I loved. I didn't need this sudden intrusion of feeling for a girl I knew nothing about. Yes, I had written her name in a mirror out of the blue. That was strange, admittedly. But it had been rubbed out and nobody would even know it had ever been there. I knew I should do the same with this new, raw desire gradually stirring within me like a volcano waiting to erupt.

Rationally, I told myself this shouldn't be happening. I was bound to another girl and happy about it. Why disturb things? The trouble was, I *was* disturbed, hugely, and the uneasiness, or whatever it was, would not go away. I needed this situation like bad breath. Whether I liked it or not, I was being pulled out of my comfort zone and having to deal with monster feelings. I was in the grip of a magnetic force but one that certainly did not come from her. If anything, she was aloof. What was it then, this Sheila phenomenon? Hilburga came to mind, and I remembered how I was suddenly engulfed then. Could that one-night Continental explosion possibly happen again? Surely not – this girl came from Fife.

At college, it was impossible to ignore Miss Cowan. She was the cynosure of all eyes, my own included. I was being drawn towards her, almost imperceptibly at first, but gradually and inevitably, and more and more strongly, as day followed day. I was now playing good parts and wanted nothing more than to concentrate on doing a decent job of them. I remember rehearsing for *Oedipus Rex* and wishing I could really tear my eyes out. Then I might stop seeing her face everywhere.

'Astonishing! This boy will go far.' That was the headline in the *Daily Express* after my performance in *Family Reunion,* a T.S. Eliot play in which I played the lead. It was my first ever press notice. Instead, I genuinely wished I could go as far away as possible. Anything to get this girl out of my head.

Here I was, happily learning my trade under good theatrical tradesmen, already broken in to professional work with the Fraser Neal Players in the summer break. Having found my path at last, I only wanted the peace to jog along it at ease, but now, once again, sex had reared its intimidating but irresistible head. It had to be sex, not love. Surely we can't love two persons at the same time. Or can we? My fiancée and I had grown up together, we had everything in common: background, religion, our friends, the same friends who nudged us together at the beginning, with nothing being said but looks exchanged and whispers made until we were an accepted item in our albeit limited social circle. It doesn't sound the most exciting matchmaking, but it was true and good and both of us were comfortable with it. We were exactly right for each other. Suddenly, I was in danger of throwing away a genuine treasure for the sake of some evanescent possibility arisen out of a fluke mirror congruity.

Alright, I had written the name of a total stranger on a dressing-room mirror. What was so amazing about that? Quite a lot, actually. It was the speck that became a spot that became a stone that became a boulder that became an avalanche and changed the face of a mountain. That's how Nature works. And we have a whole universe around us to prove it.

The human body is an ongoing area for skirmishes. Something is always at war with something else in the playful tournament of genes, hormones and molecules, and just occasionally it can get serious. This was just such an occasion. Bloody John Carlin, for mentioning her in the first place, but John was merely the unwitting agent. I myself was the pro actor and I knew I would have to do something – and soon. Final graduation was approaching and an uncluttered mind was needed. Should I just toss for it in the old Glasgow tradition? My own head was chasing my tail here. I couldn't pray about it. I felt too guilty. There was only one honourable course of action – have it out with my fiancée.

I did so on a long tense walk while seeing her home from a visit to my mother. The journey from Parkhead to Riddrie had never seen so far as we mumbled about the situation between long pauses until, when we reached her gate, she exploded, pulled the ring from her finger and threw it in my face, almost shouting through choked back tears: 'You told me to wait until you come out of the Air Force. I waited. Then you said, better wait till you graduate. So, I waited. What do you want now? To wait for your old age pension?'

With that, she opened her gate and ran up the garden path. I followed, protesting, but the front door was slammed in my face. I turned away and slowly walked back down the path, picked up the ring from the pavement and headed for the main road and the long walk home. I felt miserable about myself and sad for her, but I took a deep breath and tried to think it was all for the best in the love game.

The Greeks have four words for love: *storge* meaning affection; *philia* meaning friendship; *éros* meaning erotic and *agápe* meaning unconditional caring for another person. That's what I felt for Sheila Cowan. I felt all of these for my ex-fiancée but I didn't know the Greek word for *passion* and that's what I wanted to feel for another person. I found that I hated myself for doing so.

Going up Duke Street towards Parkhead Cross, I saw a large rat silhouetted against the night light with its hind legs on the pavement and its front paws reaching up the drainpipe against the tenement wall. I watched it scuttle up the pipe at remarkable speed. Was it running away from something or towards it? Either way, I knew how it felt.

Fourth Interval

I Speak Anguish

I speak anguish,
The world's most-spoken language.
I don't remember learning it,
I just picked it up as I went along.
Everybody has a smattering of it
But I soon became an expert.
I was misery-literate early,
A sad-face cum lauda.

But then, somebody said something,
Or was it a smile?
Or was it a look in the eyes?
It took me by surprise,
Like summer thunder,
And no wonder,
I couldn't speak, just a sigh
And I
Felt a lift of the heart
And the start
Of a long, contented silence…

CHAPTER SIX

Following Your Star

If you follow your star, you cannot fail to reach a glorious harbour.

DANTE

I WAS GIVEN A wonderful platform of parts at the first final year Public Show at the Athenaeum in May 1953 and was fully expected to walk off with the main prize, the Gold Medal. So much so that afterwards, the reporter from the *Evening Citizen* interviewed me, thinking I was sure to have won. Instead, once the judges had deliberated lengthily, it was deservedly given to Mary Ellen Donald for her brilliant cameo as a maid. She had one short scene, I had three leads, but it was not to be for me. The journalist's face was a picture of sympathy and he turned away to look for Mary Ellen.

'That's the way the cookie crumbles,' he said.

'That's show business,' I said with a shrug.

I have to confess, all the same, that I was surprised – and deeply disappointed. I had wanted that medal badly. It was to be my Gold for drama to match my Gold for art, one for each of my parents. At least that was the idea. Ah well, so much for good intentions. What was it that John Lennon said? 'Life is what happens to you while you're busy making other plans.' However, I didn't come away empty-handed. I shared the Alec Guinness cash prize and won a year's contract to start at the Citizens Theatre in the autumn, so I had no real complaints.

Better still, I started rehearsing the very next day with the Wilson Barrett Company. That was the best prize of all – a job. I tried to forget about the medal, but one of the actors in the company, Walter Carr, told me that the chief judge at the Public Show was Wilson Barrett, my new boss. According to Wally, Mr Barrett is alleged to have said of me, 'That boy's big-headed enough as it is, if we give him Gold he'll be insufferable. Anyway, it will do his character good and prepare him better for theatre disappointments. But he's got the right stuff, I'll admit, so even if we don't give him them the medal, I'll give him a job.'

I tried to put my ego behind me because I now had a future to look forward to. I was in the actors' carriage and I was on a train going north-west on a dream passage for me. I couldn't wait to get moving. The first stop was Aberdeen. It was Coronation Day 1953 and while they crowned the young Queen in Westminster I faced my first night audience in His Majesty's Theatre, now hurriedly renamed Her Majesty's Theatre in that city of Northern Lights. I felt a huge surge of optimism. I was young, fit, free and brim-full of enthusiasm for what I had chosen to do. I felt I could tackle anything and did so with a *brio* that was so often mistaken for ego.

Of course, I was self-centred. It was a necessary tool in the actor's trade, not to show off or preen, but to utilise every aspect of self in the service of professional pretence. This entails knowing oneself totally and thoroughly. No self-pretence, nothing hidden even from yourself, using every aspect of your own bodyworks, mental and physical, to play somebody else for a given time on a stage. It is playing in every sense. What other job, except football or professional tennis or golf, lets you *play* for a living? I was already earning more than my father, but on my mother's advice, I didn't tell him that.

Being an actor is to be a liar – or at least two-faced. You have to match your inner self to your outside face and pretend to be someone else con-vincingly. It is a working duality that troubled the ancients. Plato wondered how could any true discipline have any worth if it is founded on a false-hood. Aristotle, however, thought otherwise, and wrote the first play for Thespis, who had stepped out of the Greek chorus to become the first actor, and we have had thespians ever since. A play is written in the study by a playwright to be performed on the stage by actors. It is not a literary work. Even Shakespeare wrote his plays as blueprints for live dramatic action witnessed by outsiders who happily pay for the privilege. In doing so, they salute all actors as members of the *second* oldest profession in the world. I was proud to be following in that long, long line.

Theatre is unusual in that it is indeed practised by people who pretend to believe what they are saying in performance to an audience that also pretends to believe what it is seeing and hearing. This willing suspension of belief benefits both parties. It provides the necessary catharsis, a beneficial effect that is emotional as well as intellectual and it is this process that may be termed the healing lie.

I had assimilated in my training all the necessary practical stages that had to be gone through in any artistic life. First of all the artist has to *aspire*. He must have an aim, a goal and he has to go for it with every resource in him. To live by art alone, whether dramatic, musical, literary or pictorial is a luxury, and he has to earn that right, he has to *perspire*. He has to work, to break the sweat on his brow to get the effects he wants on stage, at the keyboard, at the desk or at the easel. This means he must know his medium well and continue to learn every aspect of it. This can lead to the third and final stage, where, if he's lucky, he can *inspire*.

For the actor, that is to affect an audience by what he has done in the work. He also needs the same inspiration to go for the highest level of contact possible, where nothing is said but everything is understood. After that there is nothing left but to *expire*, but he needn't hurry in that respect. All I knew then was that I was having fun on the Wilson Barrett tour, where I shared a dressing room with the oldest actor in the company, an actor who had actually worked as a boy with Sir Henry Irving. This was inspiration plus a magical link to me. I couldn't hear enough of his stories. And was wholly in awe of anyone who could reach back to theatre's first knight.

The whole, happy summer season too soon ended. Mr Barrett wanted me to play Romeo but I was contracted to the Citizens to start in September, so it was back to Glasgow to begin the winter repertory season at my favourite theatre. Repertory at that time entailed a change of play every three weeks and that meant a wide variety of casting in different styles of production over a contained year. This was a perfect post-student progression for me, with good juvenile parts in every play. My acting cup felt close to brimming over. I was not only following my star, I felt I had caught up with it already.

If God is love, then Theatre was my God. It filled my entire being. It occupied all my days and nights, except Sundays, with no thought of anything else except the joy of a new play with all that meant in new discoveries, new colleagues, new ideas. Every day was a blessing. I was a member of a rare confraternity of devout thespians who, at that time, had no film or television ambitions. We were content in our flesh and blood theatre domain, with good houses every night except Mondays, two shows on a Saturday and an extra matinée on Wednesday when required. It was hard work, but I never noticed. There was something of interest at all times, and I still found it hard to believe I was being paid for it.

However, I do remember that the first thing I did that first September morning when I reported to the Citizens was to go up to the crowd dressing room and check the mirror. Was it only my imagination, or did I still see the ghost of a name there? As I stood looking at myself in the long mirror, I remembered what had happened between Sheila and me during that momentous final year at college.

I suddenly remembered, as I stood in that dressing space how deep my feeling for this lovely young Fifer had become by then, despite the fact that frustration set in and things became tense. Both bloods were up and would soon be spilt if something didn't happen soon. I was learning even more that love is vital to being. It stirs things in the psyche that are more than physical and go right to the root of the self. The important distinction to be made is where one is 'in love' or merely 'loving'. There *is* a difference. To *love* is to yield to one's own feelings. To be *in* love is totally different. Here, one deals with another's being and it has to be absorbed completely – their smells and tastes, their wholeness as a person. One accepts the other and together they fuse into twin identity, the phenomenon known as lovers. They have a common identity. We can't consider one without the other. This is what I learned from Sheila. It had to be real.

Real love is empty of everything except love and can flourish on its own branch as long as it is tended. The parties involved grow with it and, as far as possible, co-ordinate their progress by sustained awareness of the other, step-by-step, stage-by-stage, as they inch along the branch towards the flower. All this implies a maturity of judgement and total unselfishness, which few young people have, so mistakes are made and misunderstandings abound. It was no different for Sheila and me.

Everything was against us. I was doing well at college but I had no career as yet. Sheila was only 18 and still a first year student; I was 23, a Catholic, and she was not. I was a big city boy (or rather a boy from the big city); she was from a mining village on the other side of the country. I had already been engaged to one of my 'own kind', as was said then. And she had a similar understanding with a boy who was of her 'kind'. It all looked impossible.

So I took decisive action – I invited her home to meet my parents. I needn't have worried. My dad was won over completely by her ease. Sheila's striking appearance had long been a useful asset for her, so she never feared the social occasion. My mother was less forthcoming. She had liked my first girlfriend enormously and was obviously sorry that I had broken up with her. Or rather, she with me. All my mother said to me after meeting Sheila the previous night, was, 'She'll hiv tae turn.'

'Mother!' I said in exasperation, 'We're nowhere near anything like that.'

'Oh, aye, ye are.'

'What do you mean?'

'It's in your eyes, baith o' ye.'

'Mother? I'm telling you –'

'An' I'm tellin' *you*.'

What she had meant by 'turn' was that Sheila would have to change her religion were we to marry. There was no question of my becoming a Protestant; she must become a Catholic. Things were as rigid as that in the early '50s. Glasgow was a city of two cultures, inbuilt Protestantism and incoming Catholicism, and each equalled the other in fiery fanaticism because each feared for its own survival were the other to gain complete control.

The most-asked question in my growing up was, 'Whit school did ye go tae?' This was no educational enquiry, but a blunt religious check. If you answered with a saint's name you were out. A state school, however poor scholastically, always got the nod. Indeed, some Catholic parents deliberately sent their child to non-Catholic schools in order to enhance their offspring's chance of a decent profession. Alternatively, the question was, 'Are ye a Billy or a Tim?' This referred to King William (or Billy) who won the Battle of the Boyne in Ireland when he led the English Protestant forces in their victory over the Irish Jacobites in 1688, quite forgetting that King Billy's army was financed by the then Pope in Rome. The Tim is an abbreviation of Timalloys, a rhyming play on the 'Bhoys' – the nickname for Celtic Football Club. The stark placing of opposite religious loyalties on them and their great rivals, Glasgow Rangers, has been the cause of much dissension and a few murders down the years. Yet at the start of football in Scotland, towards the end of the 19th century, there was no such partisanship between them. Football was begun in Glasgow by Queen's Park in 1867, but they were mild Protestants of the better sort and tolerated religious difference as long as the chapels kept their distance from the kirks.

It was not until the arrival of the Belfast shipyard workers in Glasgow during the First World War, bringing their William of Orange banners and Ulster flutes and drums, that a virulent stream of bigotry entered into things and permeated every level of Glasgow life. These imported workers settled in Govan and supported Rangers, the local team, causing them to recruit only Protestant players. This created further animosity between the clubs. Celtic responded by flying an Irish flag. Rangers retorted with the usurpation of the National Anthem as their war chant. And so it slipped down further into the wrong sort of rite, beginning a tradition, on both sides, of poor history, bad politics, stupid posturing and hysterical reaction that persists, though perhaps not as strongly, to this day.

The great divide was not only between two football teams in Glasgow, but ran down the centre of the country between the mainly Protestant east and the largely Catholic west. This was because of the move to the east by many during the 19th-century industrial revolution when coalmines opened up across the lowlands to feed the new factories. Sheila Cowan's own family was a case in point. They were originally Colquhouns from Loch Lomondside, but became miners and followed the work across country to Fife when new coal fields opened up there. What is ironic was that the original founding family might have been Jacobite Catholics a century earlier.

The Catholic population of Glasgow, on the other hand, was due almost entirely to the Irish potato famine of 1845–51, which cost the lives of a million Irish farm folk and caused a million others to flee the country. Most came across the Irish Sea to Glasgow, Liverpool and Cardiff because it was the cheapest escape from starvation, and, like immigrants anywhere, settled where they landed. Some braver spirits ventured inland as far as

Manchester which remains half-Irish to this day, But like Glasgow and Liverpool it's a city of two halves – Light blue or red – City or United. You can only be one or the other. Football still reflects our ability to take sides. It appears we can't resist confrontation at any level. If you're Irish, blarney only leads to barney in the end. My lot came to Glasgow and, like the rest, brought their Papist religion with them. This antagonised the Protestant Scots, especially the employer classes with their Masonic loyalties. 'No Catholics or Irish need apply' became a common notice. Why are all these old, rusting barriers still put up between Papes and Proddies? The time is surely past for such dated differences. Religion has a lot to answer for. Suspicion and mistrust joined to create uncertainty, which led to fear, which finally caused downright hate of all things Irish or Catholic.

Now Sheila and I were already feeling the thin end of this unpleasant wedge. Marriage was unthinkable, even though neither of us had as yet mentioned it.

It had emerged generally in a skirting, jocular way, especially when Sheila was pursued by a very personable scion of the House of Scone in Perthshire, who brought his brother and sister to vet her in the Station Café near Queen Street in Glasgow. They were lovely company, but I think they had the feeling that Sheila was already spoken for.

'He's very nice,' said Sheila afterwards, 'but he's not for me.'

'Who is?' I asked.

'That would be telling,' she said immediately and directly.

And I saw at once in her eyes what my mother had seen.

Something was in the air and we both knew it. Life keeps knocking at the door. If the door is locked against it, it goes to the window. You can't keep it out. This was brought home to each of us one Sunday afternoon a few weeks later as we were walking up Sauchiehall Street. A well-dressed older man put out his hand and stopped us on the pavement, saying, 'Excuse me. I just wanted to tell you both that if I were a Minister, I'd marry you two.'

Then, with a smile, he raised his hat and moved on, just as suddenly. We looked at each unbelievingly. I grinned and said, 'Well? Would you?'

'Would I what?'

'Marry me?' She looked at me steadily, then shrugged.

'Why not?'

And so on a winter's day of snow I travelled by bus into another foreign region – Fife.

I braved a snowstorm to travel alone to the far east of Scotland, to Kirkcaldy, to ask Sheila's father if I might marry his daughter. We met in a pub and over a few beers watched a televised boxing match and talked of every other thing other than the matter in hand. I returned to Glasgow with a thick head and the vague feeling that, while explicit permission was not forthcoming, neither was a ban imposed. I took that as a tacit 'Yes' and so a marriage was arranged. I had braved an entry alone into enemy territory and felt I deserved my right reward. Sheila was unperturbed. She knew her own family.

'They'll come round,' she said. 'Give them time.'

I did, but they hadn't by the time we set a date – Saturday 29 May 1954. It was the last day of my first full season at the Citizens Theatre and I stood at the altar of St Aloysius Church in Glasgow waiting to give Sheila Parker Cowan of Kirkcaldy my name. It was to be a very private affair, no guests, no big party, just the two of us and a priest in St Aloysius, her adopted parish church. Being in the centre of the theatre digs area off Sauchiehall Street, it was the actors' church in Glasgow – the landladies there making good use of their large, multi-roomed apartments. On her own initiative, Sheila had gone to St Aloysius to take 'Catholic lessons' from Father Dempsey, a Jesuit, and she was not far away from being 'received', as the official term had it. She had, as my mother put it, 'turned'. This was an immense gesture on her part. I was much impressed and very grateful.

As for our hopes for a quiet wedding, of course it never turned out like that. The *Daily Express* heard about it and, in return for the sole right to pictures, offered to pay for the reception at the Royal Hotel in West Nile Street, next door to the Italian café where we had sheltered from the rain the year before. My own kin blithely ignored our request for privacy. They could not be kept away and turned up to fill one side of the church like an Irish army. Even my lovely Protestant cousins came. Being the understanding people they are, they sat on the bride's side of the aisle, to give Sheila support.

What was best of all, however, was that the whole Citizens Theatre Company turned out *en bloc* to represent Sheila's family. Their Musical Director at the time, Arthur Blake, played the organ, and Paul Curran, one of the few Catholic actors I knew in the company, agreed to give Sheila away. Brother Jim came up from playing football for Portsmouth to be best man, and Sheila chose a friend from college, Meta Reilly, as her bridesmaid. We were fully cast, at least. I also felt I had the backing of the billion or so Catholics around the world. We were there to participate in the celebration of matrimony in a beautiful church before witnesses, but the atmosphere, at least at the start, was more temporal than spiritual.

Every wedding day belongs to the bride and I felt bad about the Cowan family's not being in the church. After all, a wedding, like a funeral, is the ultimate family occasion. They were obviously good people and I liked Willie Cowan. Why were we not in a Catholic church in Kirkcaldy?

Then Sheila appeared, coming up the aisle on Paul's arm. Here she was, only 19, yet poised, clever and capable and brave with it. She was virtually alone among strangers in a strange church with no one from her own family near her, yet she stood tall, smiling and enchanting. At the moment of 'I do', I remember I spoke out with such a thrill of pride and assurance that it drew a ripple of applause from the theatrical side of the congregation. Sheila smiled under her face veil and I was even more certain that the right thing was being done. My whole being swelled to take in the moment. Everybody cheered us outside as we got into the car (provided by the *Daily Express*) and quite a few people were on the church steps, including dear old Uncle Eddie with his usual cap on, and my favourite Swan cousin, Margaret, who gave me a wink as we drove away.

I don't remember much about the reception except that my likeable Uncle Phil got drunk on the white wine. He thought it was a kind of lemonade. I have no idea when the new Mr and Mrs John Cairney retired to their hurriedly rented basement flat near the university in Oakfield Avenue, but we both had enough energy to begin creating our first child immediately.

For the first time in my life, I felt 'manned'. I was properly armed and ready for the battle ahead. I was now multi-cast, that is, playing other parts in the new drama that life was, rather than the solo I had become used to. Being a husband was the first challenge, but I felt sufficiently rehearsed in life to cope with all the new responsibilities it entailed. Being a husband is a formidable status by any standards, but it's one often undertaken too lightly by young males. It is not until they dive in that they find the water a lot deeper than they thought, but they soon learn to swim.

There was no doubt I felt different. I was 'married'. That is, part of me was given over to another human being to be shared with her, as she gave part of herself to be mine. It was more than a body exchange; it was a psychological transfer as well. I wasn't sure I had the capability to live up to such demands. Sheila wore the wedding ring and this testified that she was now legally a person known as Mrs John Cairney. I wasn't suddenly Mr John Cowan. Why does she have to be enlisted in yet another certificate as if she were my property? She was my equal: indeed in many ways, she was my superior. All I knew was that she was now my wife, not a piece of matrimonial furniture.

She was the designated companion on the journey I was now ready to embark on as a fully trained, professional actor and apprentice husband. We would both keep an eye on the road and I was confident we would get there, wherever we were meant to go. The wedding ring didn't signify her place as a trophy or a prize, although she was certainly that. The ring represented the bond that bound us for life – at least that's what we promised at the time. And we meant it. A wedding day is not the time to be trivial about such things. What happened to us on that May morning was real and genuinely felt.

Of course, it was joyous and uplifting. We were two young bloods now joined, and the immediate result was exhilarating. Sex was on the menu as daily fare, but it was also the making of love by two people in love with each other. A necessary condition for the best effect. Sheila revealed an almost immediate maturity, in her woman's way, which nicely hid my own lack of marital experience. In other words, we got off to a great start and that augured well for the race ahead. There no doubt would be tears, but there would also be a lot of laughs, for Sheila Cairney née Cowan had a sense of humour.

Tears are for the dead, smiles are for the living.
Laughing is for children and love is for the giving.

My little couplet sums up what was the biggest event in our lives to that date, a happening so full of super-confident, happy anticipation for each of us. We had begun the process that would soon bring another, whole person into being. I was, at this time, unashamedly in a dream place, in mind and body. Who can blame me for hoping that it might last as long as both of us had being? That was what was really important.

We Make Our Mark

In the third quarter
We make our mark
Not in the dark,
But in the rose light of our years.
No fears
Now of making a bad impression,
No regression,
Our signature is on all our deeds.
Things begun, seeds
That now flower and ripen in the sun
Of all our endeavours.
Now is the time to reap the rewards
And work towards
The end in view,
For you
And yours
Now growing fast around you.
They sound you
Out for your opinion,
Where once they challenged every word.
How absurd
That time can decorate the past
And give it colours
We never even knew.
We didn't shirk,
It had to be done
By someone,
Or the edifice would come crashing down
Leaving only the frown
Of the looker-on,
Always the first to criticise

But whose eyes
Were never open to the vision
We had.
We cannot live these hectic years again.
So bid them now a fond 'Amen'.

CHAPTER SEVEN

Home Work

I will not change one golden dream/For all your dreams of gold.

PHILIP MAX RASKIN

THIS THIRD LIFE phase is really where things get earnest, where all the training and preparation come to an end. The apprenticeship is over and we have to show our worth in whatever field we elect to play in. This is where we find out if we can do it, if we are going to be third time lucky. It is an uncertain area in every respect, because the emotions kick in. We are into the practical realisation of the dream. Dreams are *very* important. They occur when the brain clears out all the debris of the day in sleep. They can also be coded messages from the ever-working brain to help the body deal with imminent decisions. We need our dreams to help us survive. A dreamless sleep is not always the best sleep, because we need that ongoing nocturnal action to help keep the brain in good order. All dreams are forged in the mind. The steel of reality is first made there.

Some people keep a dream diary. It can be a veritable lifesaver if we interpret the dreams correctly. However, we have to be quick about it. Even the most realistic of dreams dissipate into the morning light, before we have time to get to the bathroom. And a whole panorama of living information as well as wonderful imaginings can disappear in a flush of cold water. Never mind, there will be other dreams to come home to, once the day is done.

Each day is vital at this stage. It is important at any time because no two days are exactly the same. However routine we might think it, each 24 hours has its own colour, atmosphere and identity. We start again each morning and have to allow the day to make its own change of wardrobe. It takes time so see that we, ourselves, are in our work, an integral part of our particular environment. The new day, from dawn to dusk, is there to offer its own punctuation to the grammar we set out. This could the best day we have ever known, or the worst. It could even be our last. Each dawn is different and it hints at the day to come, but we never know. That's the relief. Which is why we hope for the best. And the best way to deal with it is to seize it with both hands, and not let it go until it is time to sleep again.

At this stage, we are into the serious business of living and that means applying ourselves wholeheartedly to the matter at hand. We set our target and we go for it with lance raised and at full gallop. There is no other way in the tournament pageant that any life is, never mind a theatrical existence. We must stretch ourselves to the limit, and only we know what that limit is. Theatre's many colours can be misleading and the spotlight blinding, but its rewards are great. Not only in financial terms, but also in the freedom that success gives one to pursue the idea. This is a luxury in any profession, but to be able to make flesh of something intangible set down on a piece of paper, work on it privately then sell it as a living memory to a public audience is indeed a high privilege. It is a risk, of course. Although it is one worth taking, as any actor will tell you.

What is best is that the actor works for the here and now. There's no point in working for posterity. I've never known an artist of any quality who didn't work for today – or at least for the end of the month, when there are bills to pay. Posterity is none of our business. It's a matter for a future generation and doesn't concern us. If we live now, in the present, with our only concern being for contemporary success and approval, then we are likely to pass on higher standards of peace and content to future generations, which is the only altruism the working artisan needs.

Anyway, what point is there in posterity? All art works for its own time and it's to its eternal credit that it can be valued even more by people beyond our time. Who knows how they will be living, what they will like or dislike? Will live theatre even exist in those other worlds yet to come? The stage actor's efforts only belong to the time of performance, for even the best film or television replays are not *live* and that is the essential component in theatre's flesh and blood world. At least, for the stage thespian, the truth in the moment is the aspired end despite the ever-changing scenic environment in which his or her action takes place.

If the self we were were the self we *wear*, we would no doubt change it every day as we do our underwear. But the self isn't interchangeable, it is a constant we are stuck with it no matter the poses we shrug off or the little pretences we grow fond of. The self is interior, it comes from within and its voice should be listened to. Unfortunately, it only speaks when spoken to, and most of us listen to anyone else other than ourselves. We can debate with others, argue our case, make a point that is entirely biased and even wrong-headed, but our own voice won't brook any discussion. It states what is, because it comes from the gut, which finds it hard to digest lies and pretensions. What people forget is, like anyone else, the inner persona for the actor is the real person. The outer image is only the façade, the dressing, the exterior show that gets him noticed or ignored. He understands this duality and knows he has to live with it.

In any life, the end is always seen as a dream, a hope, an ambition. It's the spur we all need to do anything. Living the dream is everyone's idea of heaven on earth, but for the freelance it can be a purgatory at best, and a hell at times. It is feast or famine from one week to another, but the compensations are many. This is where emotion applies. A full house of rapt faces happens in a theatre when the audience is moved, that is, emotionally involved. The 'house', as the audience is called, has become a home and the moment lives secure in it until the curtain comes down. Why is this so desired? Because there is love in it. What a pity the audience takes away all that love in little packets, which they can treasure as personal memories of particular occasions. They should scatter it in the street as they leave.

The world is only as large or small as we make it. It's not a matter of size or distance. The 'where' is not important, it's how we 'are' at any time, in whatever place that determines our sense of fulfilment. We have to 'be' at all times, wherever we are. All I knew then was that I was two days married, living in a basement with a beautiful wife and a boiler that wouldn't work. Help came in the form of my father, who turned up in brother Jim's Sunbeam sports car. Jim had bought it with his first earnings as a footballer with Portsmouth FC and had left it in Parkhead for Dad's use. Now Dad stood on the doorstep, waving a telegram in my face. Like everyone else on our street, my parents didn't have a phone, so I had often received telegrams asking me to ring about acting work. In which case I would go into Effie Reid's fruit shop at the corner and call from there. If I didn't want everyone to know my business I walked up to the Post Office at

Parkhead Cross. This time, however, it was personal delivery and Dad had opened it.

'It might have been important,' was all he said.

It was, but before I read it, I asked Dad to look at our eccentric boiler for me.

'Never miss a chance, dae ye, John?' he said as Sheila led him to the kitchen.

The telegram was asking me to report to the BBC at Queen Margaret Drive in Glasgow to discuss an appearance in a play to be televised from the Lime Grove Studios in London. Rehearsals to start in Glasgow during the next week. This was it. My passport to the Capital had arrived. An opportunity is only there for the taking. I took it. Looking back now, I see that this London beginning was the platform that catapulted me into the next decade of work. The said television play led to a children's series, which led to a lead in a television play, which led to my joining the Old Vic at Bristol for possibly the happiest two years of my professional life which, by the way, also saw the birth of my first child.

Everything so far had come to me very easily – including fatherhood. Surely life couldn't be so accommodating? Starting a family was a lot easier than starting a career. Perhaps it's 'not what you do, it's the way that you do it.' The old song has meaning still but I didn't have time to dwell on it as my mind was solely fixed on how to best approach a career as a professional actor, bearing in mind that he is lumped along with acrobats, airline pilots and jockeys as an uninsurable tradesman.

It's the uncertainty of consistent work that is the problem. That's what makes any stage career a challenge. 'Career', however, has two meanings – one, which is the considered progress path from apprenticeship to pension, reviewed and rewarded at given stages, with a watch, or similar trophy, awarded at the end. And, two, it is an improvised, headlong rush along the first path available and going off in any direction offered, up, down or sideways without plan or foresight, trusting in luck to reach the end. Most actors know only too well the second definition. They said of me in the dressing room that I was a lucky bastard. However, we have to make our own luck, and we can, if we have the right disposition and the tools at hand and the chances keep coming. I had the supreme self-confidence of the young, based entirely on not knowing any better. I knew nothing yet of the practical mechanics of survival.

Yet I never fretted unduly. For no reason at all, I was always sure things would work out somehow. As my old Aunt Sarah in Baillieston used to say, 'He's looked after, that boy.' I was a true optimist from the start. I was always sure something would turn up. And it did.

For instance, I remember around that time Sheila was tested for a screen part, and got it but declined to do the film.

'Why, for God's sake?' I asked her.

'Because I might be pregnant?'

'Already?'

'Are you surprised?'

I immediately hugged her to me, whispering in her ear,

'Whit's fur ye, will no' go by ye, as my mother would say.'

So she came to Bristol with me as a member of the company and mother-to-be. I had signed for a season with the prospect of another with the London Old Vic as a follow-on if required. It was a flattering contract but a challenging one; Sheila would play as cast. We both felt like surfers, riding the high wave fearlessly with no dread of any hollows that may suddenly appear. We could both jump if need be, a rocky path held no terrors for either of us, although Sheila increasingly became more preoccupied with her 'boiler baby', as she called it. Even so, she still had time to appear in a play with the company before Christmas, and at parties, we sang our duet version of *The Foggy, Foggy Dew*. It was as happy a time as two self-centred, self-contained and self-supporting young adults deserved, and we made the most of it.

There were some very good memories in that first season and I was grateful. For instance, I was rehearsed in *The Crucible* by the playwright, Arthur Miller, a precise, scholarly man, who knew exactly what he wanted. I found it hard to concentrate on the notes given me by the celebrated American because at that time Mr Miller was married to Marilyn Monroe. Another was the fight I had in the Green Room with Peter O'Toole. I have no memory of what caused it, but we were rolling about on the floor in a frenzy, being careful nevertheless not to hit each other's faces. It was just young lions' stuff, I suppose.

Altogether this Bristol span was a honeymoon extension for the Cairneys. I was on a high-octane level of learning, and revelling in it. Sheila did what she could when asked, although her concentration was moving more towards the growing interior action rather than acting on stage, but our current state of being was good. I was allowing my acting craft to be carried forward by its own volition. I was content to play and rehearse and play again and watch Sheila's tummy gradually enlarge. Jennifer announced her presence during the run of *The Merchant of Venice* and that February night I had to dash to the Bristol Maternity as soon as the curtain came down. How proud I felt in seeing my first child in the cot among so many cots.

Despite the sense of being a first-time parent, the performer in me always had the priority. There always seemed to be something in the diary that needed immediate attention, and consequently I had to leave Jennifer in Sheila's full maternal care. Ideally, parentage ought to be in tandem, and I know I missed out on a lot. But there were compensations for the actor-parent, especially on those rare good nights when everything works, when the audience is drawn in and is up there with him on the stage, as much as he is down there living in each one present. Everyone in the theatre at these times shares a deep, caring silence and, often, there is no need to say anything.

Actors call it 'velvet', for you can walk all over it and never spoil the atmosphere. I was to work a whole career before I could attain that response and properly recognise what a thrill it was. At such moments you know you are doing a good job, and that you are indeed making a real contribution towards content in others. The reward is in the doing of it and nobody needs praise for that. The knowledge that it had gone as rehearsed was enough, and to hear a fellow actor say, 'Good one, mate,' was all the confirmation you needed. To know that you had helped plant a memory in everyone there on that special night was enough. The actor's gift is his giving of his artistic imagination to the audience. Even in the extreme of tragedy, it finally offers joy.

The actor is, at base, a memory maker. He leaves an imprint in the mind of the spectator that can remain there for years. The career actor can keep his scrapbooks up to date, write his memoirs or give a talk in the local library, but it is what he leaves of the live performance in hearts and minds of others that is important. Audiences store such events in themselves.

This is what gives the actor his true status, and not all the material rewards of celebrity or fame – even fees – can match that rare distinction.

The Theatre Royal, Bristol, is the oldest working theatre in Britain and I knew I was lucky to be a part of that long tradition. However, unknown to me at that time was that other forces were working behind the scenes. As in every life, there are swirls and undercurrents that suddenly rise to the surface and change everything.

My first sense of this was hinted when I learned that Mrs Dodds, the talent scout for the Rank Organisation, had spotted me, first as a student at college, then at the Glasgow Citizens – and now she had caught up with me again in Bristol. Apparently she thought I might be film material, but was worried about my voice. Not my accent, she pointed out, but that the husky element in it might not sound too good on screen.

Despite this reservation, it was agreed that as soon as I was free I would report for a screen test at Pinewood Studios. This was a new development. I had never given much thought to films or television. I was a stage animal first and foremost, but I was also a husband and father, and as Christopher Mann, my agent, pointed out, I could do theatre in the winter and films in the summer. Celluloid was reaching out and threatening to smother the greasepaint. I was seriously tempted, for despite all my big talk, my endless theorising and my professed love of an ancient craft, I was a prostitute at heart. It was an indisputable part of the actor's psyche.

But before all that, Sheila had thought it was time to reach out to her own family again. She knew the time was right. The baby would make all the difference. So, without even warning them – 'It's better that way,' Sheila had said, our priorities were set and I had to take our lovely baby and show her off to her grandparents. That was an order. All professional decisions were put aside while we planned the big summer break return to Scotland to see the grandparents. Sheila had her priorities right. With babies, family comes first.

I took farewell of our Clifton flat and of the theatre itself because I knew in my heart, that after two seasons, I would not be back. The chance was there to go on to the Old Vic in London, but that temptress, Dame Film, had whispered that there might be something in reporting to Pinewood as requested – like quadrupling my annual salary, for one. Sadly, I had to forget that I was a well-intentioned theatrical bore and recognise that I was a married man with a wife and family.

Our Ford Popular broke down at least three times on the long and tedious trip to Scotland, no motorway drive then. The Bethlehem trio, as we seemed on the long trek, arrived weary and bedraggled at the Cowans' front door in Kirkcaldy in the early hours after daybreak. The new grandfather greeted us in his dressing gown.

'My God, it's Sheila ower the back,' he said, lifting Jennifer high.

That meant that she was the spitting image of Sheila, which indicated full acceptance, although old Willie did say when he heard that Jennifer arrived during *The Merchant of Venice*, 'Thank God, ye didny ca' her Portia.'

I liked that and I liked him. His was a rough and rowdy welcome that didn't conceal his true emotion. The whole family, mother, two young sisters and a wee brother seconded this. They didn't have to say anything; their reaction was self-evident. Willie and I left the women to it and my father-in-law motioned the red-eyed actor to follow him upstairs. He motioned me into the main bedroom and, going to a cupboard, took out a bottle of good Scotch.

'Tae wat the bairn's heid, ye ken.'

It was very early morning but I couldn't refuse and there and then we raised a glass to Jennifer. Willie sat on the edge of the bed and motioned me to the armchair: 'Ye'll be knackered.'

I couldn't deny it. I nodded, feeling the life-giving dram trickle down my throat.

Before leaving Fife I had to declare a new garage open in Dunfermline, the first hint of a gathering commercial fame after a couple of television appearances as Branwell Brontë and Edgar Allan Poe. I was only too glad to agree to the garage opening, for the fee was a new Volkswagen saloon. All I had to do was report to the garage, sit in the driving seat for a picture and drive it away. I did so through an extremely modest crowd. Mr Cowan bought the Ford from me for £400 in cash, a very inflated price, but I knew that was old Willie's way of giving us, or rather, his daughter, a delayed wedding present. I knew I liked Willie Cowan from the start and the firmness of his handshake as we parted at the gate next morning told me it was mutual.

One sad moment on the return trip south was my accidentally leaving my jacket over a chair in a restaurant in Leicester where we halted for lunch. It wasn't until we got home to Cookham that I realised I'd left it. I didn't miss the jacket, but in its pocket was my wallet, and in the wallet was Mr Cowan's cash! Four hundred pounds! I exploded, but Sheila was as calm as ever.

'You'll just have to get that film contract,' she said.

My screen test at Pinewood amounted to little more than an extended photo shoot in a studio with a very amiable photographer and later, I was called for a long interview/conversation with one of the directors, Earl St John. Despite his name, he was a very pleasant, laid-back man.

'You've been busy, I see,' he smiled over the top of Mrs Dodd's notes.

I nodded. Finally, he said he was happy enough about my prospects as a film actor. He wasn't worried about my voice.

'It's your trademark,' he grinned. 'Every film actor has one, or should have. It's that little something to remember you by. Picks you out from the crowd.'

I was duly signed up for my first film and my Leicester loss was soon forgotten.

I drove home, listening to *The Archers* on the car radio and thinking about buying that house in Cookham Rise. I sang along with the *Archers*' rum-te-tum signature tune and, for the life of me, I couldn't think of anything that was wrong with my life at that moment.

This is when being is beautiful.

Fifth Interval

Nostalgia for a Tenement

It's a sordid, derelict wasteland now
Where not even weeds will grow,
But I did – on this very spot,
Many years ago.
For here once stood a building, proud and clean and neat;
Now there's no trace of that special place in the rubble at my feet.
But I can still remember, once upon a time...
What's to remember?
Let me see...
Who was that wee boy that once was me?
In that concrete canyon, asphalt vale, already cut off and beyond the pale,
Survivors in a common band, secure in their Never-Ever land.
My urban tribe, my city clan,
In the townscape scene of my childhood's span
Where many happy days were spent
In a noisy, crowded tenement.
Now it is rubble, my boyhood home,
Nothing of it left but a vacant space devoid of grace, of all dignity bereft;
A playing field of litter, garbage-strewn and bare
And only the ghost of a building now haunts the empty air.

If I close my eyes I still can see, through the mists of memory,
That man-made mountain, brick beehive,
A warren of homes that was once alive;
A carousel of families going up and down
A tarmacadam village in the middle of a town
A living mural drawn in blood on a greystone city wall
A generation's history now lost beyond recall,
And if they and it have turned to dust.
So in the end must all of us...

CHAPTER EIGHT

Child's Play

The past is history, the future is a mystery. But today is a gift... to be grasped and made the best of.

ELEANOR ROOSEVELT

CHILDREN, AT EACH stage of their growing up, stand as markers of the parents' own history. All offspring should be named Janus, for they look backwards and forwards; backwards to the ever-widening trail they have behind them in blood ancestors, and forward to that spiral of hope we call the future, when they will advance the bloodline even further. What a lot of hope goes into such a small bundle, but this is the atom from which the next family explosion will come, which is why it deserves every care and attention.

It is my sincere belief that there aren't enough large families. If there were more children in the world and fewer adults, it might make for a better balance all round. Large families take care of themselves, more or less, and they are certainly worth any toll they might take on public welfare, for generally speaking, they produce a better product. When the house is full, everyone learns to take care of each other and the individual is able to find what resources he or she will need to assert their own personality beyond the front door. They have to find out fast who they are and deal with it among their siblings. What better training before going out to meet their other brothers and sisters out in the world? Children from a big family understand what Oscar Wilde meant when he said: 'Be yourself; everyone else is already taken.'

Parents see themselves reflected in every action of their offspring, hence the frequent use of that household phrase, 'When I was your age...' Their reaction to their children tells us as much about the parents as of their reproduction. The parental wonder at the fact of birth itself is an affirmation to them of how clever they have been to create life; their joy in the first years of their children, a tribute to their good taste in unleashing

123

into the world such an attractive human species; and lastly, the justification, on seeing their child find its legs.

Very soon the school child takes over and in no time becomes a teenage omnivore with cascading needs that can exhaust the average parent. Even as it is perplexed by its own emotions, it still asks to be reassured by its creators that they have an unending supply of love and understanding to see it through the swamps and rapids that await it on its panicking splash into young adulthood and a life of its own.

My own children never liked my big voice, the one I used on stage, and also on those household occasions when I thought order demanded volume. It didn't always do the trick, but it brought immediate silence that gave everybody time to think. However, the voice in its *piano* version came into its own at bedtimes. Days can be tiring for even the most energetic little ones, and the anticipation of a quiet night gives the adults something to look forward to at bedtime. It's a watershed time, but it had strong cultural possibilities as well. Things are laid down in the minds of little ones by stories told or songs sung.

We should tread warily as parents and consider well what we leave in our children's minds just before they sleep. Personally, at these times, I often felt younger than the particular child I was dealing with. They would often come up with a comment or reaction that seemed to come from long centuries before.

'Has the sun got its own house where it goes to every night?'

'Who lights the stars?'

'Is it true that I once lived in mummy's tummy?

How did I get out?'

Meantime, I would be racking my brains for something trivial or mundane to say before tucking them in and getting downstairs for a pre-dinner drink.

The real trouble was that my job as a touring and travelling actor, having to go wherever the work was, meant that I couldn't be a regular bedtime visitor and children love routine. They are reassured by it and mine were a little uncertain of this occasional nursery intruder who was their loving father. Knowing I was out of my depth, I fell back on old ways by crooning slow, tuneful songs from my own early times, which almost sent me to sleep before they did. So often, those grey-green eyes that we shared stared back defiantly at me as I sang the 'Wyoming Lullaby' in my best, movie cowboy style:

Go to sleep my baby, close your pretty eyes,
Angels up above you,
Wait to carry you to Paradise,
Great big MOON *is shining, shining everywhere,*
Now's the time for
(here insert full name of appropriate child)
To go to sleep.
Close those pretty eyes and go to sleep.

The word 'moon' was stretched as long as breath would allow and they would join in, laughing. There were times though, when I would rise up and get out before that last line, leaving a beautiful child dreaming. It was without doubt the best moment I ever had as a father.

Unfortunately, I was too often away working with that firm the children came to call 'rehearsals'. When very young, they didn't really know what I did and didn't care. They only knew me as a presence that arrived at their bathtimes or bedtimes and made them laugh or cry. Sheila was at the forefront of their development at all times. What they lacked in paternal daily attendance in their early years was more than made up for in a total maternal devotion they got from the other partner in the family firm, a care that went a long way to make them the admirable adults they all are today.

By some fluke or blessing I was never to be out of work for their entire formative years. This was most unusual. Film part was followed by TV role, which was followed by stage appearance, usually in Scotland, by which time another film was on the cards and the sequence started all over again, if not always in that order. In this way, the years flew by and there appeared to be no end to our family's good fortune and their father's good luck. This was shown more than anything in the steady improvement in houses, rather than my unsteady climb up the billing.

Our domestic history was modest. In the beginning, there were the rentals – a plain, brick flat in Finsbury Park, then a more substantial half-house in Buckhurst Hill, Essex, but then I was able to move my embryo family to a real house of their own in Cookham Rise, Berkshire. Our first proper home was a modern, detached new-build with a steel frame in a row of similar houses on a hill above the railway station and only half an hour away by car from the film studios at Pinewood near Iver, in Bucks. A 'house', up until then, had meant to me an audience in the theatre, but now it had become a structure, a home for a family. I had to quickly readjust. They wanted no acting performance here, but the real thing, the man who was their father. All the same, I was often unsure which front I presented. Was I their mother's husband or the actor who told jokes and sang songs?

Thanks to the prospect of a five-film run with the Rank Organisation, I was able to obtain a mortgage, which bought the first house. However, it wouldn't be ready until I was on the third picture, which starred Peter Finch and Mary Ure. The film was *Windom's Way*, so we called our house by that name. When the local reporter from the *Maidenhead Advertiser* came to interview me, he asked why I had chosen that name. When I told him he said, with a grin, 'Good job you weren't filming *Bleak House*!'

I was now skimming along quite happily. It was all go and I went. First to Corsica for my inaugural film, *Ill-Met by Moonlight*, with Dirk Bogarde. He was to be a big part of my early film career. This film paid for the down payment on the mortgage and confirmed our new status as safe risks at Barclay's Bank in Maidenhead. By sheer diligence, and some good fortune, I had attained respectable citizen status, although a respectable status is the last thing the actor seeks. That belongs to people who wear suits. This can be attained by diligence to work and that is not the first quality of a jobbing theatrical pro. My standing as a father, however, was threatened many times by the demands of the career. The provider was always at war with the performer. But what else could I do but answer the telephone? It is the actor's trumpet call to arms. Sheila could never understand why I persisted in my ingrained priorities. It was often a hard choice and she could only watch with an increasingly stern face. In her eyes, I was far from being an ideal husband. But I could be a good father, however unconventional. Although even that was severely tested.

Like when I was working on *Ill Met By Moonlight*; Sheila was in

London that day and I was on standby while babysitting Jennifer. I was suddenly called into the studio for a reshoot.

'But I'm baby-sitting.'

'I don't care if you're squatting on the roof, get your arse over here, pronto.'

I had no option but to get out the pushchair and take Jennifer with me. I came on set pushing it and good old Dirk Bogarde, who was on the set at the time, had the presence of mind to wheel the pushchair away while I did my solo retake.

I probably did my best work on the film in that sequence. I was to chew on a stalk of grass as I looked down from a supposed high viewpoint in Crete, commenting on what I saw or heard on the road in a series of one-liners, which were later dropped into the film as required. It was maybe only half a dozen sentences, but that was a lot of time in close-up. So intent was I on Jennifer away at the back, in case she would cry out, that I forgot to 'act' for the camera and just said the lines automatically as they came into my head. Michael Powell, the director, liked it so much that he printed the first take. I had learned the first lesson on film acting – don't act.

It was the same Michael who said to me, 'You play the costume and the make-up very well, but why do you leave yourself in the dressing room?'

I couldn't answer that. Every instinct in me was to perform, to act, and thus I drained the dialogue of all spontaneity, by thinking about it too much. In the course of the next decade I was to do a lot of film work, but I'm not sure I got any better. My whole being was geared to presenting the outside self as the character no matter the script. It was the camera that got behind the make-up. It wasn't for the want of good advice given me along the way by the big names who had their own ideas. These comments, given lightly to me in the course of filming, when put together form a practical film wisdom in their different ways.

Firstly, there was Dirk Bogarde in *Ill Met by Moonlight* and *Victim*: 'Don't think about too much – just do it.'

Then John Gregson in *Miracle in Soho*: 'Imagine your character as someone you know, and imitate them.'

And Peter Finch in *Windom's Way*:

'Think how lucky you are to be in bloody work, mate.'

Kenneth More in *A Night to Remember*:

'Look for every laugh you can get – even a smile.'

Ian Carmichael in *Lucky Jim*:

'Learn the script. It's all there.'

James Cagney in *Shake Hands with the Devil*:

'Keep yourself fit, buddy. You need to be in this job.'

Nigel Green in *Jason and the Argonauts*:

'Listen hard to the director, then do your own thing.'

Richard Burton in *Cleopatra*:

'Just think of the money, boyo, but get back to theatre when you can.'

Burton's was the one comment that stayed with me longest and I was to put it to the test – but at a later stage. I came to the conclusion that the best way for me was to read between the lines. That's where the inner, true narrative is. What is spoken only hides the meaning at times. Perhaps I should have gone to the Actors Studio in New York where they churn out film actors, but no, I went where they train all-round performers who prefer to appear before people instead of lenses. This preference, however, didn't stop my appearing ultimately in a score of films in all the London studios, but I don't think I got much better by the end.

I had something of a track record as a stage actor, but found I couldn't transfer the physical technique to that required for the camera. I was so self-consciously aware of being photographed, of being held in shot while static. The element of stage acting that I missed was of constantly moving, not striding across the stage, but responding with every muscle to an actual living audience at that time, who were assembled specifically to hear the whole story.

In film acting we are given pieces to play with, shards of actuality which are mere fragments of the whole to be assembled later. And yet the good film actor can give seeming life to these disparate moments, so that, in the end, they make a believable whole. I was playing the bit for all it was worth and not realising its relevance to the whole thing, which, as far as I could see, was only in the director's mind.

What makes it all the more difficult is that on the first day of the film, you can shoot the last scene. There is no such thing as an ordered sequence as far as character development. In other words, it can be factory acting, where you are given your orders to supply the material required. Only the very best film actors are able to do this on request and do it to the highest standard. This is what Sir Michael was trying to tell me.

The basic element in film work is that it really is a minute of panic surrounded by the hour of lethargy. That call to camera comes just when you're about to finish a crossword or are in the middle of an anecdote with another actor in the next canvas chair. Suddenly you have to wrench your mind away from happy, practical reality to the concentration required to play the most offhand or trivial line; or even more difficult, to deliver the crux emotional moment of the film. The skill is in delivering the powerful charge required on the word 'Action' from the director. On stage, we had left the director in the rehearsal room and, supplied with all that was learned there, we were able to complete the two-hour traffic in the sequence set down by the playwright. This gives the stage actor the benefit of incrementally building towards the emotional climax.

I had always felt easy on stage because I was well rehearsed and for the most part well directed. On film, however, the more 'in the moment' you are, the better your effect, which is why the really good film actors always have some little something in reserve that makes even the smallest interjection sound spontaneous and real. The good film actors exude a sense of fully 'being', the lesser ones insist on 'acting', and I thought myself in the latter bracket. Why then did I get so much film work? I was 'castable', I was told by a casting agent. I wasn't sure what that was, but I didn't question it.

I was just glad to be asked – often enough to move up the house ladder as each child appeared. When baby Alison appeared, we moved to *Fawley*, a delightful little bungalow in Maidenhead. Now, almost three years later, I was in television between films, helping make a series in Cardiff for the BBC, *Barbara in Black*. Sheila rang me one February evening to tell me that Lesley Susan Helen Cairney had arrived.

'What's in a name?' is the well-known phrase, but actors could tell you how important a name is in show business. My own name was not considered commercially viable. Several agents had advised me to change mine and even at college, the Director, Colin Chandler, said my name might be a handicap.

'People can't immediately see it,' he said. 'Nor can they spell it.'

When I told my father this, his reply was typically astute.

'If they can spell Gielgud,' he said, 'they can spell Cairney.'

Meantime, I realised that I was missing the audience I could see from a stage and not on the other side of a camera. Fortuitously, I got a call at home from Glasgow. It was Callum Mill, an actor I knew well and liked, who was now Director of Production at my old theatre, the Citizens. He had a problem. The actor who had been cast in the forthcoming *Hamlet* was no longer available. Was I free to take his place?

'To play what?'

'Hamlet.'

'*What?*'

I was on a sleeper train that night to Glasgow!

Sixth Interval

What is Age?

Age is a stage we're all at – more or less,
Chronological punctuation that makes its own sense
Or nonsense – depending on how you feel,
Or how you look. Or how you think you look!
Yet what rage about age,
What tears about years
That mean nothing but dates in a calendar.
And even there, 'Time' becomes another page
To be rip'd out quickly
To serve as notice to the milkman,
Or make rapid calculations to pay bills.
Your age
Is a page always lying open,
Your diary of survival,
A tablet for Fate to make its scrawl,
That's all, a testament of tenacity.
When you have no age, you haven't lived
Or have just died!
But you are LIVING – and ageing,
Even as you read this.
A few more rings on the bark,
A few steps upward on the steady climb
Towards better things,
Or yet another stumble down
To things we're scared to think about.
Perhaps it's this fear of an unknown age
That makes us wince at every birthday
But if we looked inside ourselves
We can see there is no age.
As any sage will tell, at the centre of all
Is nothing – or everything...

CHAPTER NINE

Finding New Solutions

To everything there is a season.

ECCLESIASTES

THE GREAT QUADRILATERAL for all male thespians is the Shakespearian foursome – Romeo, Hamlet, Macbeth and Lear. They all come with the same age differential that marks this book. Romeo for youth, Hamlet for early manhood, Macbeth for maturity and Lear for old age. That is indeed the compass of man in dramaturgy. Now I had the chance to play the prince of parts. I had played Romeo, albeit at college, but then I was exactly right for it at that age. I felt I was now, at 30, in the correct Elsinore state of being. There was no way I was going to resist the opportunity, no matter what it cost me in lost fees or name-making on the big or small screens. Everything was put aside as Shakespeare took over. So, taking a deep breath, I made for my hometown and the Glasgow Citizens Theatre.

The first night of *Hamlet* passed in a blur, but the audience reaction was wonderful. When I began the famous soliloquy, 'To be...' the audience responded with a muted but united whisper, '...or not to be.' I nodded in agreement, and continued, 'That is the question.' I never did say 'or not to be'. And not one critic noticed. Shakespeare had so much to say about what I am trying to convey here, that is how best to cope with life in all its swirl:

Whether 'tis nobler in the mind to suffer
The slings and arrows of outrageous fortune,
Or to take arms against a sea of troubles
And by opposing, end them? To die, to sleep –
No more; and by a sleep to say we end
The heartache and the thousand natural shocks
That flesh is heir to?

The three-week run was a complete sell-out, especially the extra matinées. It was such fun, and not at all the solemn Shakespearian experience I had anticipated. Not that I didn't remember it was a tragedy. The play was still the thing. Director Callum saw to that. I knew, however, by the end of the run, I had just won the long jump, and was mightily relieved. This was something that lifted me as an actor into another plane.

Yet, the one memory that I have of it to this very day was at the close of a school matinée. Hamlet dies at the end, or almost at the end of the play, with the line 'The rest is silence...'. With Callum's agreement, I had the idea of cutting the word 'silence' and instead creating a silence by stressing the sibilant carried over from the 's' in 'is' and so ending in a hiss which faded naturally on the breath. It worked a treat and got the required deep silence from the audience. However, on this one particular performance for schools, a young girl's voice, or so it sounded, called out tearfully from the balcony, 'Oh, don't die!' It was the best response any Hamlet could ask for. I was thrilled. It was October 1960.

As an actor, I knew I had just come of age.

Afterwards, work offers continued to come in, especially on television and films made for television. 'A whole new field of unemployment has opened up for us,' as Michael Redgrave, a famous actor of the time, put it. I could almost pick and choose what I did, but I knew it was all within that narrow calibre of casting known as 'type'. I was becoming known as an intense performer with a comic potential and a usable singing voice. There were plenty of roles in this range but the Hamlet experience had disconcerted me.

I had almost forgotten the vibrancy of stage acting and the vital part the audience played in making the experience memorable. I nagged Barry Krost to find me more theatre. He, justifiably, protested that as an agent, he only stood to lose if I continued to be snobbish about work. He couldn't let go of the gravy train while it was still running smoothly.

'I can't live on gravy, Barry, I need some meat to get my teeth into.'

'Tell you what, Johnny boy, you give me another film and I'll get you a dab of grease paint.'

Once again, he was as good as his word. I did another forgettable film somewhere then Barry rang to ask if I were available to play Captain

Absolute in *The Rivals* in London. This was West End stuff, although at the Lyric Theatre in Hammersmith, and it came just at the right time. Sheila worried that I was doing too much and overwork might prove just as costly as no work. I could grow stale and lose enthusiasm or worse, get sick and have to cancel jobs.

'No chance,' I told her. 'I would sooner shoot myself.'

Sheila immediately retorted, 'Knowing you, you'd probably miss.'

We were now arranging our next new house, the much-loved *Fawley* in Maidenhead Court having been exchanged for a dull, modern construction called *Highways* opposite Maidenhead Cemetery. The baby machine was still in perfect working order. Now school claimed them. For the older girls this meant the posh Brigidine Convent in Windsor, all nuns and children in white gloves, straw hats and blazers. Meantime, the absences from home went on. All of which may have cleared the mortgage and paid the school fees, but it put a strain on my paternal status, not to mention husband and wife relations. The career paid no heed to such niceties.

However much I might pull against the work front, it pushed harder and I couldn't resist. I still couldn't say no to any offer. I never knew where it might lead. Perhaps if we knew what was coming we might never do anything, just let it all happen as it will, and take what comes. That was not my way. I wanted some control, even if it was only my two hands on the steering wheel. I had resisted playing Scots in my career as I thought it would typecast me in character roles and I would find myself imprisoned up a tartan cul de sac. I was confident that I was leading man potential, now that I had made a successful London debut in *The Rivals*. I got excellent personal notices in the big Sundays, as the *Times* and *Observer* were called, and I felt that my career had peaked.

Then life intruded and returned me to a more proportionate view of things. During the run at the Lyric, I was advised to return quickly to Glasgow as my father was very ill and might even be dying. This news put public acclaim and press notices in their proper perspective and my stand-in went on while I flew back to Glasgow. It was indeed a matter of life or death and it concerned my father, so there was no hesitation. He had been ill with stomach problems before but things had turned serious and he was now in Glasgow Royal Infirmary.

I was surprised to find him surprisingly cheerful and not at all discomfited. But he was bored with life. Or so he said.

'You don't get ulcers from boredom, Dad.'

'I know that, but I'm no' doin' proper work. Keepin' a scrapbook for you an' Jim is no' whit I'd call a real job for a grown man, is it?'

'It's not meant to be a job, Dad. It was just something to keep you occupied between the golf and the bowls. You don't need to work, you know. Jim and I – '

'Oh, I know. You an' Jim are dain' fine by your mammy an' me. But it's no' aboot money. It's mair than that. It's havin' something tae dae. Somethin' worthwhile. Every man needs to work at somethin'. Look at you, you're run aff yer feet, but then your's isnae a real joab is it?'

'We don't need to go over that old stuff, Dad.'

'Right enough. Ah, I know whit I should've done years ago. I should have stuck wi' the music – but that's a by wi'. A' the same, I cannae tell ye how much I regret it. Regret's a killer, son, it eats away at ye, ye know.'

There was a long pause. I felt like I was 12 again in London. This was so untypical of my father. But of course he was seriously ill.

'Are you afraid, Dad?' I asked at last.

'Of whit?'

'Dying.' I hated even saying the word.

'Not a bit,' my father retorted with some spirit. 'Let's face it, son. Dying's the last great adventure. Or the first? Have ye' thought o' that? Anyhow, as soon as I go, I'll *know*.' He cleared his throat. 'I could do wi' a drink.'

As I gave him water from a tumbler, it spilled down his neck.

'Christ, son, ye'd make a helluva nurse!'

Those were the last words I was to hear from him.

I left him sleeping and went back to spend the night with my mother. She was resigned.

'Ye should stey oan. He'll no' last. He thinks he his nothin' tae live for.'

'He has you.'

She said nothing.

I flew back to London next morning and was back on stage that night giving a very empty performance. My father died a week later, on 3 April

1963, just after the run of the play finished and for the first time ever I was out of work. To be honest, I didn't care. I had gone for nearly a decade non-stop and it ended when my father died. Why was that? Was it mere coincidence or was it to give me time to grieve?

My father's death hit me hard. Much harder than I expected. A son doesn't become his own man until his father dies, but I could have waited. I didn't want him to die. To hell with being my own man. All I wanted to do was to get home to Glasgow again, and quickly. I flew back in a dark suit, wearing a black tie and with a heavy heart. Dad's death reminded me of the real relevance of things.

It felt odd to be fatherless. I had seen so little of my dad, really. Only in early boyhood, lying on his back while he swam out to sea at Ayr, with me clinging on, or watching him lead the pipe band in the park. He cut a fine figure of a man. The neat hand he had in writing letters, and above all, his ease when sitting on the piano stool. Now that lovable, charming man was gone at only 54.

Looking from my old tenement bedroom window, two storeys up, all I could see was a lake of flat caps filling the street below me. They were the huge band of men who had come to my father's funeral. The pipe band was there, but it didn't play. Only the kettle drummer stood by with a muffled drum. The others waited with the rest holding their silence. Dad wasn't there to lead them. He was already off on his big adventure. Jim was in Canada and never made it to the funeral, so I had to comfort my mother as best I could. She was very calm and all she said about her husband's last days was, 'He never said he was sorry.'

'Sorry for what?'

'Oh, it's a long story.' Then she cried. It was the only time she did.

How was I to remember him? He had so many good faces. He should have been the actor. I remember well the good advice he gave me about how to deal with the interview, so much a part of every actor's life.

'Jist mind,' he told me when I mentioned that I had a big interview coming up about my playing Gulliver in a new series, 'Jist mind that however big and important the man behind the desk is, he still has tae wipe his ain arse twice a day.'

It was a typically terse and cogent observation from him and it came to my mind whenever I met the Mussolini types who sat against the window behind the big desks at the end of long carpets. I noticed that they all pretended to be busy, head down and scribbling, and never looked up as you came in. I did meet Mr Schneer, the Gulliver series producer, in his imposing office and my father's advice relaxed me immediately.

'Take a seat,' said Mr Schneer, head down. I immediately lifted the nearest chair.

'Where do you want me to take it?' I said.

I got the job. All it gave me was a wasted month in Hollywood, because the Gulliver series was never made due to 'technical difficulties'. I was just as glad. All I remember of Hollywood was playing table tennis – and not very well. I felt jaded. Was I still grieving for my father? I could still see the handsome face in the coffin. What I did remember though, about the funeral, was that there was one unexpected visitor. It was a woman wearing a big hat and smart clothes and speaking with an English accent. Could she see Tommy? No one had ever called my father, 'Tommy'. I was hesitant and went first to tell his mother in the kitchen that an English-woman was at the door.

'Let her in,' she said quietly without moving.

I did and led the woman to the bedroom and the coffin. I stood there watching while she looked down at the body.

'Oh, Tommy,' she said softly, and laid a gloved hand on the corpse's cheek.

I stiffened at that but then she turned to me and said gently, 'He looks so young. Give my sympathy to your mother. Thank you. I'll let myself out.'

And she was gone before I could move. Who was she? Had she really happened? I never asked my mother, but I had my own thoughts.

I then remembered my father's embarrassment one afternoon years before when I was a student. I had come home earlier than usual to find him writing a letter at the kitchen table. He quickly shielded the notepad but I noticed that the envelope was addressed to a woman in England. We had a few words but he said he owed money to his old landlady and was just sending it back. My mother's words suddenly came back to me –

'He never said he was sorry.'

137

It was eerie getting the coffin down the tenement stairway. I had the childhood memory of my father carrying my sister in a tiny white box when she died suddenly at nine months. Dad carried it downstairs as if it were his toolbox. Now it took several sturdy uncles to bring him down to street level. There was only the sound of that one muffled drum as that regiment of working men, aligned in fours, walked slowly down Springfield Road, over the cobbles and tramlines behind the hearse as I led them in that long, cloth-capped, grey-clad procession to the church. I don't remember anything of the funeral service or the internment in Dalbeth cemetery. The mind has a comforting way of blotting out painful recollections. It's a happy amnesia that allows us time to gather our mental and physical forces together again and prepare for the next of life's contingencies, good or bad. This is when the body is a friend, and every body is the same.

Back in London again, I lost yet another leading role to Alan Bates, this time in *Look Back in Anger* at the Royal Court. I got the part at the audition but lost it whilst sharing a drink with the director afterwards in the pub. I still don't know what I said, but he came to the conclusion that I wasn't really a company man. That ego impression again. All the same, I was sure of getting the next part, which was in the film *Far from the Madding Crowd*. I had the casting director on my side, but Alan had the director on his, and both of us were called to the Dorchester Hotel to meet the big-noise American producer who couldn't make up his mind between the two of us. Eventually Alan got the part because he came from Hull and I came from Glasgow. The big shot thought Alan was the genuine Englishman and I was an alien Scot, admittedly of the Maidenhead variety. Thus, geographically, Alan got the part and went on, quite rightly, to become a big star. I got a taxi back to Paddington Station.

But it was there I saw a Robert Burns poster on the wall and this gave me my big idea.

The ground for it had been laid two years before, when *Hamlet* had brought home to me the full potency of acting as felt in the living exchange of persona between actor and audience at the given moment. They each can feel, even smell it at times – the veritable pungency that tells both that contact has been made. No wage or fee can better this engulfing sense of mutuality. It makes one realise that theatre still survives as a working art form. I wanted more of it and it came up in a most unexpected form. I had done a spot for Jimmy Logan on his television show for Burns Night 1960.

In one scene, I was dressed and made up as Robert Burns and positioned as if I were his portrait in a frame. I then had to recite a Burns poem, which ended:

> Then let us pray that come it may,
> (As come it will for a' that,)
> That Sense and Worth, o'er a' the earth,
> Shall bear the gree, an' a' that.
> For a' that, an' a' that,
> It's coming yet for a' that,
> That Man to Man, the world o'er,
> Shall brothers be for a' that.

The big TV camera came so close that I could see myself in the lens. It might have thrown me at other times, but it didn't on this occasion and the result went out on air. The reaction from viewers was so good that it came to mind again when I saw that Burns poster. Why couldn't I play Burns on stage as a solo? Emlyn Williams had done so with Dickens, Hal Holbrook with Mark Twain and Micheál MacLiammóir as Oscar Wilde, so why couldn't I do so as Burns? I had lost a big film chance because I was a Scot, so why shouldn't I be a Scot? There no doubt was a resemblance. I was 35. So was Burns when he came to fame. I went home from the failed interview in the Dorchester buzzing with excitement. The film opportunity was already forgotten. It was as if it this Burns thing was meant to be.

It took me three years to move the project from an idea in my head to a practical possibility on stage. In the meantime, my fourth daughter, Jane, was born in Maidenhead. Professionally, I continued to fit in various other television, stage and film commitments as they arose. I finally opened the Robert Burns solo at the Traverse Theatre, Edinburgh, in January 1965 – and, in one way or another, have been playing Robert Burns ever since. This show has remained a constant in my professional life, with good and bad effect, even to the present day. The bad effect was that it ruined my conventional career, which at that time included a film contract with Columbia Pictures and a recording contract with HMV, not to mention various calibre television shows, including *This Man Craig* for BBC2. The good was that Burns' gave me a name, and opened up a whole world of touring opportunities.

Little did I realise that this tiny Burns mustard seed would become a tremendous tree and smother everything else in my career from then on. What began with a single poem to camera and a poster in Paddington Station became the bedrock of my career over the next three decades. Robert Burns had come into my life and he has never left it. He may have destroyed my conventional career, but he gave me whole new life. The importance of this episode is that it offered me an unexpected path, in fact, a broad highway, which I had no option but to take. It proffered opportunities then unseen and could easily have been passed over. But they weren't.

The ability to guess what may be behind signals given and to trust instinctively in the ability to navigate as directed can have the effect of changing everything in our lives and we must be ready to live or die by these decisions and the actions these decisions demand. Finally, the greatest gift of all is to be able to do what we want, when we want and how we want. This is called artistic liberty and men have died for less. It is the ultimate reward to follow our star, not to be blinded by its illumination, but guided by its light.

I had found the ultimate freedom in the solo. It had unchained me from the restrictions of conventional, rehearsed company theatre and released me from the moment-by-moment demands of the camera. I could talk to my audience. It was in fact an ongoing, albeit one-sided conversation. As I was given the words to talk to them, they were given the silence in order to talk to me. We were two strangers in the night, but bonded at the falling of the final curtain. My only wish for my fellow artists, in whatever discipline, is that in the course of their working lives, they may know the excitement as the juices inside rise up and the air is filled with expectancy. No words are needed. It is an awareness between artist and audience and the recognition of what their joint purpose is.

In the '70s, my touring demands were increasing in range and subject and even extended to cruises on ships like the *Uganda* and the *Canberra* for P&O. I added my solo Robert Louis Stevenson and Robert Service to the play list and with them, charged here and there – and charged for it.

My only response to the guilt I felt about being apart from the family for so much of the year was to pile on the 'stuff' and the luxuries. But wiser friends, like actor Roddy McMillan, warned me that I was doing too much and might pay for it.

'For God's sake, take a break, man,' he said. 'Try sayin' naw, for once.'

But 'Yes' to everything was a compulsion. As long as I was free I was ready to go with it, whatever it was, as long as it carried a feel and all expenses were met. As a working actor, that's what I did after all, and I was carried along in the general euphoria. I was at my peak, physically and mentally, or so I thought, and imagined it would go on forever. Onwards and upwards, smoothly and easily. But it didn't. A line from *Hamlet* came to mind: 'There's a divinity which shapes our ends, rough-hew them how we will'.

My son, Jonathan, arrived in Maidenhead Hospital on 1 March 1970 – a Sunday's child, like his father. I celebrated next day by driving up to attend a Celtic football match in Manchester with brother Jim, who was visiting from Canada. As a result, I missed the photo of mother and child taken by the *London Evening Standard*. I don't think Sheila was too happy about that. She thought she looked like a single mother, but I had to take my few breaks when I got them, and football was my only relaxation. Celtic won and I resumed my happy marriage when not in a just as happy scramble around Britain with one-night stands as Robert Burns.

The years passed and the family was now living in Kellie Lodging, our large, historic National Trust property in Pittenweem in Fife. But there was no stopping the Cairney/Burns express at home or abroad until sometime in 1973, after a performance in Perth (Perthshire, not Australia) that I collapsed in my room at the Salutation Hotel. An anal haemorrhage caused blood to drip everywhere. I was really scared by its ugly suddenness. Still dressed in my dinner jacket from the show, I drove home in my Range Rover at top speed all the way to Pittenweem and collapsed at my own back door.

We Make Our Peace

In the fourth quarter
We make our peace,
Cease to care what others think.
Drink
Instead from that cup,
Now over-flowing,
Knowing
We have done our best,
Passed every test
They set before us.

We can now relax,
No longer tax
Our legs to walk,
Our voice to talk,
Our brain to think.
Sink
Instead into the warm bath
Of our attainments,
Mere entertainments
We see now.
But take your bow.
You had your time
When what you did
Could be said to chime
With what your age demanded,
And gave you, open-handed
That rare and signal power
To prize the golden hair.

CHAPTER TEN

Travelling Hopefully

If you would create something, you must be something.

GOETHE

I CAME TO LYING in a hospital bed. I was in Ward D1 of Edinburgh's Western General Hospital, where I had been diagnosed with extreme ulcerative colitis and was in intensive care. Roddy McMillan had been right. The butterflies in my tummy, part of the trade risk, had turned to scorpions over the decade and had been eating away steadily at my intestines. I was now under constant observation. Even the local press hung about the door. Were they expecting, even hoping, perhaps, that I would die? Instead, after a few dark days, which included seeing my own unshaven face staring down at me from the ceiling and thinking I would go mad through one long hour after another, my sanity was saved by the lady who came round with the library trolley.

We are all supposedly alert to the possibility of the main chance – the big break that will make us. That sounds paradoxical and even the word 'chance' itself indicates a risk. But mere chance, in other words, is the unworked-for opportunity that can arise in life out of the most unexpected circumstances, even in locations as unlikely as a hospital ward, and a vehicle as ordinary as a book trolley. But it was here I found the life story of Ivor Novello, the celebrated composer of West End musicals in the post-war years. I didn't know much about him except that he wrote some lovely melodies. What surprised me was that I immediately identified with the story of the Welsh actor/screenwriter who was capable of writing an immortal line like 'Me, Tarzan – you, Jane.'

Another idea was born. Why not a life of Novello on stage, illustrated by his own songs? With various nurses' help I got more volumes on the composer from the library and over the next weeks began to work on an idea for a one-man show with dramatic and musical assists. I was immediately engaged. There is no feeling like when the idea becomes a purpose and the purpose takes over. I was almost shivering in my pyjamas with excitement. By the time I was freed from Ward D1, with no operation done, but with a warning to try and not be always running ahead of myself, I came home with a working script and a project to be realised.

In any art, the idea is all. It is that inexplicable something that comes up our back, gets to the back of our head and infiltrates somehow to the brain, where it passes the message on and leaves the rest to the hearer to determine how to respond. Many have great ideas and do nothing about them. Others have dreadful ideas and attempt to implement them to the last letter, often causing a disaster all round. The patient observer (and I was certainly a patient at the time) uses the experience given, or things seen, or sounds heard, or any kind of visceral response that can prompt artistic movement.

This can be the setting down of the first words on paper, the first notes on a musical manuscript or the first dangerous daub of paint on the canvas. In many cases, this can send the careless executant off in the wrong direction, but with patience and diligence, the work can be completed to everyone's satisfaction, and more importantly, can improve the quality of life – however slightly. This is a high aim and deserves the best of efforts, which is why, when any idea comes unbidden, we ought to consider it well. Because when we listen without prejudice, it will come through clearly because it comes from a source much bigger than yourself.

As soon as I was fit again, I got into a quick huddle with my new manager, Colin Harvey Wright, who had come in to my life from the better part of Glasgow to become my accompanist on the piano or accordion, as required, and rose within a few days to becoming my manager. A quiet, unassuming young man, he was just the brain I needed and even better, he made his current home in Edinburgh available to me as office space and temporary lodging. Cometh the hour, cometh the man. It was a special kind of serendipity sent Colin to me. He was an unexpected anchor when personal seas around me were just becoming rather rough.

I have to confess that I have always been readier to take rather than give. But such selfishness was merely a venial sin of mine, and I could be talked into thinking of others. I prefer to think I had a proper sense of selfhood, which is just selfishness in long trousers. Be that as it may, the public rooms in Colinton Road soon became the headquarters of a new company, Shanter Productions Ltd, complete with the lovely Sue Frame as secretary. She was a friend of Colin's and married to John Frame, a famous Scottish rugby player. Sue undoubtedly added a much-needed air of cheerful, sporting efficiency about the place.

Colin and I now discussed what we might do with my embryonic Novello script. Being a musician, he had contacts at the Royal Academy of Music in Glasgow. Through them, he found two excellent female singers in their final year at the Athenaeum, soprano Isobel Buchanan and contralto Anne Hetherington. Suddenly we had a show on our hands. *The Ivor Novello Story* was presented first at the Cottage Theatre, Cumbernauld, near Glasgow, and went on eventually to fill the Lyceum, Edinburgh, and the Theatre Royal, Glasgow, before later touring very successfully in Scotland and later still, being a hit at the Edinburgh Festival.

Once again, it proved the correctness of following an idea through and keeping faith with the concept. Confidence in the project gives one the energy to pursue it with efficiency, thus guaranteeing the best results. As Ray Bradbury said so pithily, 'First you jump off the cliff and build your wings on the way down.'

I had made the jump and now here was a delightful pair of wings opening out to reveal the simple narration of the theatrical life story illustrated by songs. It certainly worked for the next decade and more. So much so, that even today, I am amazed at its success with contemporary audiences. No professional could be more complimented that something conceived, written and planned in a hospital ward should find such a long life in the theatre – especially after having its genesis through the wall from an operating theatre.

It succeeded because it was written with feeling, an ingredient that is almost mandatory in theatre work, but one that can't be taught. It has to be in you, and in your work. If the feeling is in you be sure it will come out of you in performance. That's what it's there for. In addition, there is an extraordinary satisfaction in completeness, in seeing an arts project through and realising that what was in one's own mind can now be shared with audiences. It has become an actual artefact, a living work tool. The Novello piece was a modest attainment, but it had a good story, some laughs and very singable songs and with the happy ending we all pray for.

It even has a posthumous possibility, with a potential life beyond mine, but that is not at all a priority.

Life itself is the best story of all, and we hang in there chapter by chapter, because we are all curious to know what happens. It rarely is as we expect. That's half the excitement. If we knew what lay ahead, we might not want to go. The safest way it to take as it comes and make the best of what we get. Indeed, the ideal state of living your given life is to go to bed reluctantly and wake up eagerly. Unfortunately, as we grow older, the very opposite seems to happen, but I didn't find that at this stage.

I was now the assured professional and could have taken on anything, but what I did was take, on sound medical advice, what I called a 'sicky sabbatical' to try and get my body back to working order. At least the deliberate idle spell gave me the chance to read the huge Pittenweem Bible handed in to Kellie Lodging by the local fishermen. It was the size of my bedside table, but it was kindly meant. I eased off all work as the tummy problems came and went. They were kept at bay by steroids, which did the trick but gave me a big fat face, which I knew wasn't fit to be seen in public. Nor around the house, according to Sheila, who objected to the medicinal aura that now hung around me. I bought a very expensive after-shave, but to no avail. I began to feel like an outlaw in my own house.

As soon as I began to feel even slightly better, I took the first chance to move beyond the doors again and back to work, even though my sabbatical had a few months yet to run. I couldn't keep away from the make-up. I was offered a lead part in a political thriller adapted for television, *Scotch on the Rocks* for BBC Scotland. Pharic MacLaren, the director, for whom I had worked before in *The Master of Ballantrae*, had delayed the start to allow me time to get fully fit. This was an unheard-of courtesy and was much appreciated. Every day on the job was a help at that time. I was determined to get well again, or at least get my own shape back.

In the script, I had a love scene in a submarine with the leading lady. When Maria Aitken saw me stripped to the waist, she said I looked like a pear. I replied that it didn't matter; she looked a peach. That mollified the situation somewhat and we got on with the scene.

I was also happy to escape to Glasgow and move in with my mother in Dennistoun, having moved up in the world from Dalmarnock.

Now, I was living with her. I didn't know how to tell her why I was bringing more and more of my wardrobe over to her house with each visit. I said I needed to look fresh for work. It seemed that my whole life at this time was hinged on a matter of personal hygiene and steroid shape. But what could I do about either while I was still under doctor's orders? I couldn't kid my mother, though. She asked me about it one night when she brought me a cup of cocoa to the bedroom.

'Is everythin' a'right wi' you and Sheila?'

'I'm trying to learn my lines, Mother.'

'An' I'm tryin' tae find oot whit the story is. I cannae get in tae my ain wardrobe for aw your things.'

'It's alright, Mother, I'll be away again in a couple of weeks.'

'That's no' whit I'm annoyed aboot, an' ye know fine.'

'I know. But can we talk about it at the weekend? I've got to get these words off.'

'Ye've aye got an excuse.'

This time in her new home gave me the opportunity to realise what an intelligent woman my mother was, no matter her Glasgow off-handed-ness with it. She wasn't clever in the bookish way my father was, nor had she his way with words, but she had an unerring instinct for the kernel of things and had, of course, her 'seeing', which only came to her, she said, when matters were really serious. Like my deteriorating marriage, for instance.

Which was why she was now picking at her son, in her way, hoping I would let her see behind my bluff to the marital preoccupation that she guessed correctly was worrying me. It wasn't health, despite my ulcer problems. My father had the same trouble and it killed him in the end. It wasn't money. I had more in the bank now than she had ever seen in her life. It wasn't the children, she'd never seen happier or bonnier weans, as she called them. Therefore, it must be Sheila, which she knew, too, was none of her business, but once a mother…

The mother–son relationship is an ongoing phenomenon. It doesn't end when he leaves the house, it's a birth to death reality. It's much stronger than the father-son bond, which leans more often to respect and admira-tion, rather than to the unshakeable, unbreakable love that ties a mother to her boy for life. One can only assume it's the same for daughters and their mothers. They may cut the umbilical cord but they can never sever the connection.

Yes, my mother was no fool and I knew I couldn't keep my own marital misgivings from her for much longer. Sheila was going off me. I could feel it. I knew my mother would worm it out of me sooner or later. This is where a good relationship tells. There was a close bond between us, and not just because we were family. We had had all the big rows and the mutual shouting and noise, but never tears between us at any time. This was because ours was such a fundamental love that it served as a buttress against any hurting pain our differences might have caused. I would have killed for my mother and I know she would have died for me. Not that we'd ever say such things, but that weekend we did have our talk.

I took her to dinner in my old friend Tony Matteo's Italian restaurant at Parkhead Cross, the Duke of Touraine. I had performed a few Burns Nights there and felt easy in its Glasgow-Italian atmosphere, and my mother enjoyed 'the wee sherry' before dinner. I made sure that she had a few wee sherries that night.

'Are you tryin' tae get me drunk?' she asked, with a smile. And over the spaghetti bolognaise I told her about the marital situation. Her only response was, 'Ye canna marry again?'

'Who's talking about marrying again?'

'Ye married wance and that's that. But yer no' the type that could manage single long.'

I didn't say anything but poured the last of the red wine into my own glass. My mother didn't want another sherry.

We walked home in the night air, saying no more about it. I looked up at the sky, full of stars, and wondered what my father might have said.

'Watch where ye're gawn,' my mother said with a laugh as I tripped on the pavement. She caught me by the arm, and I didn't let go of hers all the way home to Dennistoun.

With the Novello phase over for the meantime, I got back to Burns. People said this Burnsian takeover of my acting career wouldn't last, but I was to play this character off and on, in some form or other, for almost as long as the poet had lived in real life – 37 years. Of course, I didn't know that then. Had I done so, I might have hesitated. But none of us can out-guess the future, we must 'play the present', as they say in tennis. I was certainly building up the points, but I wasn't sure if I were winning the game. Sheila did write in the early stages, saying that I was ruining my career by concentrating on one character, and she was quite right, I suppose, but I was hopelessly tied to my dream – to take my world of solos around the world. The agents weren't too pleased either. They lost a lot of income. I was also making less. But at least I kept it all now, so I was quite happy as Colin and I continued our endless peregrinations around the world in the '70s.

Burns took me to New Zealand for the first time. A new epiphany was about to take place. It did so on Monday 4 April 1977, the day I arrived first in Aotearoa. This was only the latest in the big jumps I had taken in my life. The first, at ten, from wartime Parkhead to Perthshire, at 20, in the Air Force to Germany, at 30 to Berkshire, at 40 to Fife now, at nearly 50, to New Zealand, the next stop being the South Pole. I could reach out no further from my roots. It was as if fate were giving me a guided tour beyond my own life expectancy.

But I never at all expected just what was to happen now.

Seventh Interval

Goya's Old Man on a Swing

Like Goya's old man on the swing,
I feel myself blown on the wind,
Caught in the upsurge of my winter years
As giddy as the flying boy
I thought I'd left behind.

Isn't it good to let yourself go?
Fall back,
Safely held,
Impelled
By your own inertia,
Knowing that the force which pulls you back
Will also push you up
As high as you can go.

You know
This is nature's power,
Free for all,
No better fuel,
Nothing to do
But hold on,
Trusting in God's breath
To blow where it will.

CHAPTER ELEVEN

Taking the Initiative

A lying gain is a reptile which devours the speaker slowly.

ST KATHERINE OF ALEXANDRIA

AUCKLAND, NEW ZEALAND, was a delightful surprise. Small, wooden houses with coloured roofs, which were lovely to see in the strong sun. And a whole sense of old Britishness, which took me aback and gave me a feeling of belonging – a sense that I had been here before. It was a city, not a grey one like Glasgow, but vibrantly green offset with the blue that the nearness to the sea gave it. It was altogether a striking landscape and one that made me want to paint it.

The first week playing Burns at the Maidment provided me with another surprise. In the first act as I walked from stage centre to down right, the stage light covering me blacked out as I began the line 'I arrived in Edinburgh...' I quickly ad-libbed 'in an eclipse'. This got a nice reaction and covered the exigency. I then carried on with the script. Afterwards, a lovely dark-haired young woman came round the dressing room and made her way through the crowd of middle-aged Scottish matrons, there in all their tartans. Coming face to me, the young lady said calmly: 'That was very good. I liked your ad lib.'

I said, 'Thank you. One has to say something.' But to myself I was saying, 'Wow.'

'What's your name?' I asked her.

'Alannah O'Sullivan.'

'What a lovely name.'

She told me that she was an actress with the Mercury Theatre, the professional theatre in the town, and that if I wanted a late drink after the show, the only place open was at the theatre bar, as all the pubs in New Zealand shut at six o'clock at that time. I said I would love to, if she accompanied me. Would tonight do? She was a little taken aback, but before she could say anything, I explained in a whisper that the group of Scottish matrons had prepared a tea and sandwich supper for me and it wasn't what I needed after a performance. I said if Alannah were willing to give this excuse, I might avoid this crush of Scots accents and Scots fare. In fact, a decent drink in good company could be found at our production motel. Would she like to join me there? She was dubious, but agreed as the gathering was theatrical. But how to get there? Colin had taken the car to prepare for the various stage staff who were coming.

'I've got transport,' she said.

'Good,' I said. 'Any chance of a lift?'

'Sure, I'm parked outside.'

'Excellent,' I said. 'Just let me tidy up and I'll see you outside in five minutes. I'll explain to the ladies.'

Alannah left and the only reaction I got from the ladies was, 'Ye'll miss a guid supper. We'll just hae tae eat it oorsels. It canna gae tae waste.'

'I'm sorry,' I said. But I wasn't really, and hurried out to meet the young Kiwi actress, to find that her transport was a big Suzuki motorbike and she was holding out a helmet to me.

'Do I have to?' I asked.

'It's the law.'

Moments later I was holding on tightly as she sped through the Auckland streets, packed with late runners and insomniacs painting their houses in the late evening light. With my arms round her waist, I felt a wonderful surge of exhilaration. Who wouldn't?

When we arrived at the motel car park, Alannah was having doubts about joining the party, so I pointed out that she couldn't drink much anyway, as she was driving this fierce monster of a machine – and she might like to meet Colin and the stage crew. She agreed to stay for a short visit and I escorted her up to our first floor suite. It wasn't quite the demure supper party. More a louche excess of hard drink and soft drugs among people, young men and younger girls I had never seen before, in a haze of cigarette smoke and other fumes and no sign of Colin. I was as amazed as Alannah was and could only stare at the mess, but Alannah reacted quickly and was out of the nearest door before I could say anything.

Unfortunately, it was out to the fire escape, but out she went anyway.

I followed immediately and got a glimpse of her hurrying down the metal stairs. I called out, trying to apologise, but she paid no attention. When I reached her at ground level she was standing beside her motorbike with her back to me, putting on her helmet. I tried to apologise again but she completely ignored me. I then lost my patience, and grabbing her shoulders, I roughly pulled her round to face me – and got the fright of my life. I gasped and I suppose my jaw must have fallen open.

'What's the matter?' she said.

I couldn't speak for a minute, then I gasped, 'I see us married.'

She was on her bike in seconds and was off in a roar.

It was then her name came back to me and I shouted after her, 'Alannah!'

It was no use. She was gone.

What I had seen was a picture of two people standing in front of a rhododendron bush, both dressed as if for a wedding. It was Alannah and ME! Our very images. She was in white and I was in a green suit. I didn't have a green suit. As soon as she turned away the vision faded. But it was there alright. My mother's damned precognition. What did it mean? Was I being told something again? Something I didn't want to know. This girl and I had met less than an hour ago. It seemed unlikely we would ever meet again. Did I want that? She'd made it clear she didn't. I stood there not knowing what to think other than it was definitely us in front of rho-dodendrons. But that was impossible. I didn't know anyone who had rhodo-bloody-dendrons. Ah, to hell with it. I turned on my heel and almost ran back up the fire escape. I needed a drink and I didn't care what it was…

Oddly enough, Miss O'Sullivan and I met again before the week was out – and it was at her request. She rang the motel to ask if Colin and I could come for dinner at the flat she shared with another student. She said she just wanted to talk.

'What about?'

'Anything you like. New Zealand?'

Again it was that same calm voice. I wasn't sure what to think.

'Let me check with Colin. Hold on.' Colin's response was equally calm.

'As long as the meal isn't dug out of the ground,' he said.

'What are we eating?' I asked.

'Leg of lamb.' Colin gave the thumbs up.

'Sounds good. Okay. It's a date.'

Monday 4 April 1977. Easter Monday. It was to be a very important date in my life for reasons that will become evident. We did talk about New Zealand – all through the tasty leg of lamb dinner. First of all, there was nothing at all foreign about the place. Certainly Maori were new to me, and I enjoyed meeting them. But the ordinary New Zealander could have been someone I would meet in Berkshire, Birmingham or Bathgate. They made me feel so at ease, and did everything to help the tour go smoothly. Robert Burns was welcomed everywhere, especially when I wore the costume and audiences rose exponentially the further south I went. Until I was in that other Scotland, that is, the place that lay between Dunedin and Invercargill. The students in Dunedin met me off the train in a small sports car, highly decorated with tartan, and drove me like a trophy to the hotel and for a photo shoot at the theatre. I had tea with the Provost and realised quickly that I might have been in Edinburgh. I also knew I had fallen in love with New Zealand.

At around midnight, Colin left and Alannah's flat-mate went to bed. Alannah and I continued to talk at her table. We talked over the dish washing, we talked while walking in the dark up the hill behind her house and while sitting on her doorstep watching the dawn come up over the bay. I can't remember what we talked about. It doesn't matter. The words merely hung in the air between us while I fell gradually fell in love with this part of New Zealand the woman who sat on her own back step in a comfortable old cardigan, with her arms round her knees and her eyes taking in the first light of the new day. I sat beside her, in a borrowed red pullover, my shoulders touching hers, trying to remind my self that I was a married man.

Ultimately, neither of us had anything left to say.

A bracing, black coffee ended the idyll and I was quickly put on the back of the motorbike and returned to normality and a resumption of the tour.

At the end of the tour, much to my surprise, Alannah came to Auckland airport to wave me off. Was she waving goodbye or was it an *au revoir*? My feelings while flying home were ambivalent to say the least.

I arrived at London airport to find a letter waiting for me on the communications pillar. It was from Sheila. I hoped nothing was wrong with any of the children. I sat down on the nearest bench and pulled out a single sheet of paper. Yes, it was her handwriting, but what it said had me sitting up bolt upright. It was very terse and came straight to the point. She no longer loved me and wanted a divorce. Would I take the necessary action? I couldn't believe it. I was stunned. This surely couldn't be happening? But there it was in black and white. I was being dumped. I passed the page to Colin and he passed it back to me without a word. And in the long pause a very small thought crossed my mind. Why couldn't I have received such a letter in New Zealand? A certain girl and I would have had a lot more to talk about on that doorstep.

Eighth Interval

If I Had My Life to Live Over

If I had my life to live over
I'd live it, not give it
Up to safety and the sensible way.

I'd make more mistakes,
Take more chances,
Make sure my troubles were real
And not imagined.
They would then be worth the bother
If I had my life to live over.

If I had my life to live over
I would try for more moments,
As many as I could,
And I would in every fresh day
Cherish the new
Instead of always having to explain the old.

I would be bold
And never dread what lay ahead,
But take it as it comes,
Good or bad and be glad.

I would sing more loudly,
Dance more abandonedly,
Love less guiltily,
Sleep more soundly,
And waken optimistically.

If I had my life to live over
I would live it
Right up to the last gasp,
Which would not be a sigh
But a Hallelujah!

CHAPTER TWELVE

I Belong to Glasgow

... the long, long years that bow the head and turn the growing
spirit back to dust.

ANONYMOUS

OF COURSE, I OUGHT to have flown straight home, but Colin and I were due to join a cruise at Southampton that night and I would be away for six weeks. Reconciliation would have to wait. As it happened, it proved impossible to achieve. I saw my lawyer in Glasgow, who expressed surprise that I should want a divorce from such an attractive woman. I reassured him loudly that I hadn't bloody well initiated the process, whatever my feelings might be. I didn't believe in divorce, I argued. I couldn't agree. I was told calmly that Sheila was adamant and would take action herself on the grounds of desertion since I was so often away from home.

'But I was earning the money that kept her.'

'That's beside the point,' said the cool, lawyer's voice. 'Marriage is a contract that requires a physical presence as much as a standing order.'

It gradually dawned on me that there was nothing I could do about it except go back to work, if only to keep the cheques flowing in the direction of my children.

As a species we are nothing, if not resourceful. It is a quality that is at the root of our survival instinct. Given it, we can cope with anything, or at least learn to live with it. It's what makes us into hitchhikers when the car breaks down on the road and into swimmers when the ship goes down. We learn soon that we want to live at all costs and with as little fuss as possible. I had to draw on these inner assets now, as I was really on my own. Colin had to decided to put his house on the market as he was thinking about going back to university. He had had his theatrical fling and was considering marriage – to one of our Novello singers. He was on his way in as I was on my way out. I was solo again, and not just in a one-man show.

A further irony is that it took nearly a score of people to put me on stage in the Burns show. From front office to front of house, from hotel room to back stage prompt corner; it was an ongoing operation requiring forward planning and rearguard action. On an impulse I got in touch with Alannah again to invite her to play the voice of Ireland in a show I was arranging around the voice of Count John MacCormack, the tenor. But, stripped of production resources, and due to Alannah's unavailability, I couldn't get the show together, and it fell away as a no-go. I was now a real soloist – sans wife, sans manager, sans new Kiwi friend, sans everything.

The solo actor was on his own, literally. The little convoy of support that I had had throughout my career was now dead in the water: the ships, Sheila, Colin, Sue, Barry Krost *et al* had deserted the sinking rat. To all intents and purposes, Shanter Productions was rudderless. I flew alone back to New Zealand, ostensibly to do the agreed return tour of my own *Evening with John Cairney*, but really it was an excuse to see Alannah again. To make sure she was real and not just something I was imagining. Fittingly, I arrived on St Valentine's day to find on calling her number that she had left for London – that very same day! Now what did that mean? I did the tour anyway and enjoyed it, if only for the wonderful surprise I got when, out of courtesy, I visited Alannah's mother and sisters at Oxford near Christchurch. Looking out of the kitchen window on the first morning, I saw the biggest rhododendron bush I had ever seen. In my mind's eye this time, there was Alannah in a white wedding dress standing in front of it. I came back to Britain with a lump in my throat and not a sensible thought in my head.

For a man whose marriage had died, who had a suspect stomach, was technically homeless, whose office now had a 'For Sale' sign at the door, whose bank balance had been devastated and who now wasn't entirely sure who the hell he was, I was suddenly aware that I was alive and working as usual. Work was now my only mistress and I served her faithfully. I made a wife of my production company, Shanter Productions, and it bore me five simple but lucrative offspring – theatrical solos on Robert Burns, Robert Louis Stevenson, Robert Service, William McGonagall and my own stage story, *An Evening with John Cairney*. I dipped into all of these separately and collectively, to make programmes as required and a decent professional living was found. This was my new family and I appreciated the company.

I went to London to see a hotel group about a Highland tour they wanted, and, to my delight, I discovered Alannah was still there. I made contact, inviting her to join me at the Edinburgh Festival to play in my new script, *At Your Service*, on the life of Robert Service, the versifier. She was free and did so. As the weeks passed, things changed. For the first time in a year. I was no longer solitary. I had a companion, a colleague and more importantly, a friend. I was still very much in the post-Sheila phase and still feeling scarred – or was it scared? However, I got some kind of reassurance from the work Alannah and I were doing. We had found a very effective partnership with a feeling of easy proximity to boot. Alannah was revealing almost daily her many talents.

I soon saw that one of these was for administration. So I asked her to stay on in Edinburgh to look after the office while I did my next American tour. It was there she began a lifetime friendship with my daughter, Alison, who was at Edinburgh University and a fellow lodger at the time. I returned from the tour to find everything in order, and Alannah and I found that we worked well together, not only on stage, but across an office desk. I was left to ponder my good luck while confined to my bachelor attic after an office or writing day and doing any man-chores about the house. Our relationship was warm and easy but totally professional.

It was therefore a huge surprise to me, when during a countrywide snowstorm in the winter of 1978, she suddenly asked me to marry her. I couldn't understand what had made her do so, but she told me that any man who could unblock a sink, dictate a programme blurb for our Charles Rennie Mackintosh show, drive across Scotland in a blizzard to see his children in Fife, his mother in Glasgow and return to her on the same day, was the one for her. Besides, she knew I'd never get around to asking her.

By now *The Ivor Novello Story* was on the road again and Alannah was its efficient stage manager and Narrator. Was there anything this girl couldn't do? She even arranged our removal to my mother's flat in Glasgow when the Colinton house was sold. To live under my mother's roof in the company of an attractive young girl to whom I had just become engaged was going to be a challenge for all three of us. Fortunately, my mother realised Alannah's qualities at once, and Alannah adjusted to her and Glasgow almost immediately. I was at home in every sense. I had wanted us to marry in Glasgow, but my mother demurred and insisted that we marry in New Zealand.

'The lassie needs to be wi' her ain folk on her big day,' she said. 'Besides, I've seen ye merrit afore.'

My divorce papers came through on 29 May 1980 – my Silver Wedding anniversary. Hi-ho, Silver! I was a free man. Free for what? There was no great celebration and I filed the papers away. I have never seen them since. Alannah and I arranged our cruise ship contract so that we could be delivered back to New Zealand, where we were married a week later than planned, on Friday 27 September 1980. And yes, in her mother's Canterbury garden in front of the rhododendrons, just as I had foreseen in that Auckland car park three years before. I was even wearing a green suit I hadn't owned then. It was a week later than we had planned because my own dear mother died suddenly in Glasgow – in the very week when Alannah and I might have married.

I flew back at once, sitting between two young girls who were also going back to Britain to bury their respective fathers. We didn't talk much. The funeral flight is something all expatriates have to consider. I was able to see my mother in her coffin, but I didn't recognise her. Her hazel eyes were closed. Those eyes that saw through me but told me everything. My mother was my first pal, my closest friend, my hardest critic, but she was also my constant support. I miss her yet. Leaving the flat and my mother's affairs in my brother's hands, I about turned and flew back to Christchurch.

I was now parentless, but I had a new life anchor in the former Miss O'Sullivan, who was to steady my psyche and take us both not only round the world, but into a new world of shared trust and total satisfaction in every respect. As one South African lady remarked on one of our many P&O cruises, 'I can't believe you two are married. You look much too happy.'

We were, and still are.

Alannah was right. I would never have sought a second marriage, but now that I was in it, the sensible course was to accept it, give wholly to it, and take advantage of what it now offered.

Alannah became an effective co-performer with me in the Burns and McGonagall scripts, as required in their new duologue format. By utilising her obvious acting talent, we split all my solo scripts down the middle, especially the Stevenson, giving half of it to her as Mrs RLS. In return, she gave me half of her Dorothy Parker script as Robert Benchley and another couple of shows were born. I was part of another family now and it was called *Two for a Theatre* and our motto was 'Have Script, Will Travel.' We applied the same formula to my scripts on Robert Service, Oscar Wilde and Lord Byron, to which she added Jane Austen and Shakespeare and I countered with my wartime script, *Blackout* and the nostalgic song/script *I Belong to Glasgow*. When I added my solo extempore offerings, we soon had a very workable canon of 23 duologue playscripts, which we could market and present as required anywhere and everywhere, wherever an audience was to be found.

This now became our main employment under the Shanter Production banner and with this extensive word haul to call on, we travelled around the world over the next few years utilising well-paid P&O cruises to carry us over oceans between continents, either taking us to New Zealand or bringing us back to Scotland. We had our adventures in many lands, survived storms and hazards, enjoyed the sheer luxury of liner travel, saw the Grand Canyon, went into the pyramids and visited most of the big cities of the world, making many new friends in different countries, amassing a cartload of memories along the way. The whole thing was *esprit* and we enjoyed it as such. I wish theatre could provide more of this kind of evening for audiences and for the actors' sake. It is a formula of trust, and if played honestly, it never fails.

We travelled through the '80s on a wave of continuous work that took us, by courtesy of the Arts Council, British Council, the English-Speaking Union, Keedick Lectures and the university circuit in America to everywhere where English is spoken and many places where it wasn't. It was a wonderful experience that not only bonded us as performers, but as two people. There is no closer relationship than that occasioned by a 24-hours-a-day togetherness.

New Zealand, of course, featured regularly. So much so, that in the '90s we made our home in Auckland, and I became a very willing New

Zealand citizen, enjoying operating from that lovely country for nearly 20 years. In that time, I discovered academia, and got myself a doctorate on RL Stevenson. I began writing in earnest, and had a book a year published, and finally found painting, having two selling exhibitions and winning a national art award. We also bought a kitten and called her Calliope. And there in two pages, you have in outline the somersault my being took in my maturity, and no one is more surprised than I am that I landed safely – back where it all started for me, in Scotland, 84 years ago to the very day.

Scripts have been written, shows done, cups of coffee downed, wine poured, rubbish told at the dinner table with dear friends and family, painting rediscovered, music listened to, more books published, football matches have been watched and religion renewed, and life is now enjoyed to a degree I never thought possible. I see now that I made my children with Sheila but now I make my days with Alannah.

I said earlier that every life was a story, but I see that it is more like a story within a story within an even larger story and so on to a bigger one still until, like a series of Russian babushka, it goes from one small box to another bigger box to an even bigger box until it culminates in a story so big that it can only be considered in terms of mystery. Our development is clear from local development to regional awareness, on to national identity, then international status and finally universal acceptance before we merge into that Unknown that is the enigma of the Cosmos.

Modern cosmological thinking appears to suggest that in the incomprehensible, unthinkable antiquity before Time began there was nothing, or what scientists prefer to call nothingness. However, behind that nothingness, in a dark mass of the unknown, there was an energy of some kind, a cause, a reason, an idea that created the effect that was the aboriginal source of all things and the very beginning of the first universe. Scientists call this element dark matter because, as yet, they don't know what it is. But it's the band of gravity that surrounds our earth and holds us all together.

It is assumed that a singular event of unbelievable magnitude, possibly or probably occurred among a sea of galaxies many, unthinkable billions of years ago but in the mid-17th century it was believed that the Bible held all the answers. James Usher, his Grace, the Archbishop of Armagh, concluded in 1654 that the Earth had been created on 23 October 4004BC. He arrived at this precise date by adding up the aggregate ages from Adam (whom he says was created on Day Six) through the genealogies of every Bible protagonist that ever lived and arrived at his own mathematical conclusions. However elementary his sums, this would give the world's age in our own era as 6,017 years, which is surely the biggest understatement of all time.

The trouble with all theories is that they are merely opinions backed up by whatever contemporary information is available, but this information keeps changing in every decade. We have to keep reading to keep up with it. Watch this outer space. Whatever way we jump, it would seem that we jumped first out of the frying pan into the fire. Modern science, or the proven cosmological reality, reveals that we are descended from the same matter that produced stardust, that we are all, basically, stars. There is no need to look further than into ourselves to find our star. In our own make-up is the wherewithal to create whatever we like. We can look again, see what is there and make of it what we will. That is the only way to justify the gift of heart and brain.

Everything we know of the world today came about complete in the instance of that ultra-remote pinpoint explosion in space. If nothing will come of nothing, still less will something come out of a vacuum. What is nothing, after all? You can't see it, touch it, feel it or even imagine what it might be like. That is why there are so many controversies related to our universal origins. Why can no two minds agree on the prime issue: how and where did it all start – or the even bigger question – why? Nothingness is not nothing. If reason applies at all, there must have been *something* before time existed – a starter of some sort, surely. It stands to reason, that is, if reason still applies in this perpetual debate. It appears that whenever scientists pull back the curtain on our beginnings in space, they seem to reveal yet another curtain and yet another beginning.

I am now back where I belong, among my own in the City of Glasgow, and revelling in the awareness of being in the right place for the time that I am at in my life. I rise to a morning of writing which spills into an afternoon of painting, which, in turn, spills into a wine glass if I'm not due out that evening, and I raise a toast to another working day. I would not, I could not, have it otherwise, and please God it may continue for a while yet. Yes, I'm growing older by the hour, but all I want now is to keep on doing it.

People reach out to help me up stairs, or down, as the case may be, just because I am so obviously old. But I am not in any way decaying – deteriorating perhaps, but not decaying. While I appreciate the kindness of strangers, I want to stand on my own two legs for a while yet. There is nothing strange about getting old, although it does seem unfair that we are punished physically for surviving. First the hair goes, then the memory, then the hearing, then the legs and so on through this once proud temple we call the body.

Second childhood is part of this same natural process and is so given that we might approach our end as fresh as we were at our beginning. All of nature works in cycles and we are no exception. It's the lure of the lair, the hearkening back to the smells of the nest, to that place, wherever it was that we called home. That world we knew once, that was comforting and protecting and not daunting and challenging. In short, making a homecoming is to come back looking for love. It is always the last word in these speculations.

What I recognise now, however, is that it all started for me in Glasgow and it is still there for me now that I am back. I never pushed to return. I was pulled, strongly and irresistibly, back towards my beginnings. It is a powerful magnet that drags us back to our birthplace, the first important place in any life. Alannah feels the same about New Zealand as I do about Glasgow and the West of Scotland. It's a natural, topographical or geographical bias towards a particular place. This is the element that today has become twisted into that hyper-nationalism, which, when twinned with religious bias, is the cause of so much unrest and, in too many cases, wars. Nevertheless, an association with place in its basic sense is the confirmation of a deep, all-round connection exuding warmth and comfort and it is this that carves the deep niche within all of us that never lessens.

Whatever the reasons, there is at least one really important place in all our lives. It could be a school, our first holiday resort, our first cinema, our honeymoon hotel. Any one of these could be the picture we carry in that small pocket of our mind where it has lain undisturbed for years. This is why we can become quite sentimental about bricks and mortar, or stretches of sand, or trees on the side of a mountain, whatever and wherever it is that marks our particular memory place. I have four. A quartet of very different places: Glasgow of course, for all the obvious reasons of family and nurture; Edinburgh for its theatre and cultural links at the Lyceum, the Assembly Halls at so many Edinburgh Festivals, concert recitals and all the hectic activities of the performing arts; Berkshire for a succession of beautiful houses paid for by a series of not-so-beautiful films and television appearances; and finally, Auckland, New Zealand, for the gulp of fresh air it gave me in mid-life and for the peace of mind found among a secure second family that allowed me space in my mind to think of getting a doctorate, writing books and rediscovering an under-worked talent for painting.

I had come back to Scotland annually, not only for Burns appearances, but also on book business. In 2006, I was due to make several book festival appearances in order to publicise my then latest book. One of these book readings was at Wigtown in the southwest of Scotland, almost on the English border. It was a lovely date, a lovely town and Alannah and I made a holiday of it. Book festivals are good for the ego. Nobody says a bad word about you, and every title is a winner, at least during their specified tent time. The hospitality is first rate, because, being bookish, everyone knows the necessity of a good wine at the table. In addition, Wigtown is made up of bookshops, streets of them, and with my bookish inclination I loved that. The printed word, bound and decorated, has always been a thing of beauty to me, and no machine with a screen can match it.

Wigtown, therefore, was a pleasure and I was sorry to leave it and take to the road again in our borrowed Range Rover, a gesture from my English son-in-law. Stewart is really a Geordie from Newcastle, so perhaps he is neither English nor Scottish, but only my son-in-law. The drive up the west coast of Scotland en route to Glasgow was a delight in the sun. It was a beautiful day and a pleasant drive, even though I was driving. At one point, looking out of the window, Alannah was prompted to say, 'Would you like to come back to live in Scotland?'

'I might when I'm old.'

'But you are old.'

'So I am. I keep forgetting.'

And that was the difference. I genuinely didn't feel elderly and that was an important attitude to have as the hearing dulls and one begins to rely on glasses for reading. There's not much you can do about it and I find if I never mention it, I soon forget about age. The only time to boast about age is when we're under five and over 90. Meantime, the thing to do is live as we are. It is certainly better to look old than to feel it. Evidence of age is a badge of survival and should be worn proudly. The years of being write their own literal biography on our bodies and this physical portrait tells us more about ourselves than any biased autobiography. It is not the aggregation of days that makes a life but the quality of the moments within those days.

We are only as old as what we can do. Well, I can walk and talk, so I can still do my day job, and I keep having new ideas about how I might do it yet, and do it better, so there is still everything to live for. It is a wonderful reassurance. We cannot live anyone's life for them but we can spread our own out as far and let it touch others. People can walk all over it if they must, as long as they derive some comfort or security from the carpet it provides. This is the good use of the fibre of any life.

Age may wrinkle the skin and change the colour of your hair, but the loss of enthusiasm wrinkles the soul and discolours your view of things. Enthusiasm, as I keep insisting, is the gift of life and lasts as long as we keep interested and alert. The decision to come back to Glasgow, as soon as we had tidied up things in New Zealand, gave me another surge of this life fuel and it was the equivalent of a blood transfusion. Mortality itself is only another word for the temporary. Nothing lasts in the world. All things material have their end date already stamped and there is no getting away from it. We have our span, and that's it.

Ego Absque Finis

When our final span is run
And all our earthly deeds are done
When everyone like you and me
Is laid out there for all to see
The ego will sing out loud and clear

'Remember me? I'm still here.'

Stoically you made your way
Now it is plain you've had your day.
Accept it gladly.
If you ever had to do it again
You'd do it badly.
What you did well was well-regarded
But now lives in time discarded
Let it die
Let it die while you live
and give to the moment
And allow yourself
The blessing of the every-changing NOW.

Conclusion

It's the long, long years that bow the head and turn the growing spirit back to dust.

ANONYMOUS

THERE IS NO CONCLUSION. Human beings merely change the circumstances. Life goes on. Mine is a triumph of mere survival. I have travelled the world but only now, in this late phase, I see myself as completely at ease. I do not say this lightly. I am still in the lists, still on the road, but, at last, I am at peace, and to be at peace with one's self is more than just important, it is necessary. It is the potent part of the whole business of being.

We are all our own little worlds and tend to selfishness as a first defence. It would help if we knew better how we work best, but we keep going round and round in circles of our own making, going over and over the same tracks until they swallow us up entirely. A full life is not necessarily lived in the mainstream. We can bubble along quite happily in any of life's many little tributaries where the currents are lively and the water clean and the current goes in the same direction as the widest river. The water journey is the same.

We are each given a stream to follow that's exactly right for us and for our capabilities, but so many never see it, or, sadly, find it too late. If we trust ourselves, however, our ways will find us, although they might come in a very roundabout manner. Everything in life is complicated. Our own body is in constant motion, as busy as any road works or railway system, things going up and down, in and out, stopping and starting, going at speed, and all to the rhythm of the heartbeat or on a signal from the brain. It makes its own song. The wonder of all this is that with so much going on at the same time, so little goes wrong. Life is a song to be sung lustily. Just pick a key that suits.

We are all in the life orchestra and even as individuals we have instrumental similarities. The metaphors are clear: some of us are in the strings, doing most of the work of the melody, others are in the brass section making most of the noise, percussive types keep us all in the right rhythm and the woodwinds are there for any embellishments. With such disparity the need for a conductor is obvious. Some think him a God but many argue that He is superfluous. The question is always open, but the living music has to be played nonetheless. Harmony is difficult to attain because we are each so attuned to our own song, that we find it hard to sing any other.

The human body itself is like an orchestra. It amazes me that a collection of disparate personalities gather together with a miscellany of bits and pieces made out of steel, wood and animal skins to collectively create beautiful sounds emanating from the mind of yet another poor mortal, and scribbled by him or her on pieces of paper. Of course it goes wrong occasionally, or is misunderstood. We are, in fact, conductors of our own body orchestra with a thermometer as baton, leading a constant symphony of voice and body parts. The working slogan is 'muscles make meaningful music'. They respond to a confident beat and won't play for a poor conductor. Of course, accidents do happen. Tragedies occur. Storms blow up. There are disasters. These are the facts of life. Not a day goes by without people being injured – a helicopter drops from the sky, an island is caught in a cyclone or we hear that someone we know has cancer. This is how sickness comes to the body, as the exception, not the norm, so we should accept it occasionally, and wait for the body team – all those hormones and molecules – to get together and cure us. Our own immune system is always our best doctor. Let it do its thing and it will make us well again. If we can still laugh, then we're still young and therefore curable. No matter how much every bone in our bodies contradicts this, it is true that we *are* only ever as old as we feel.

The mind is the master, but we don't realise this while we can still run like the wind and reach out our arms to touch the horizon. We are sometimes seduced by our own evident abilities, imagining that such powers will last forever. But we know that that is youth's greatest gift – not knowing. If we don't know, we don't care. Everything is possible and because of this innocence of knowledge, great discoveries are made. We often stumble on things accidentally, but the skill is in spotting the useful or artful within the event or happening. There's no luck about it. Someone had the wit or mind to see it. They had the dedication, the determination, and above all, the doggedness to follow through. With this kind of attitude, we can do almost anything.

Like leaving New Zealand, for instance. In 2008, it had its challenges. Our precious library was decimated. We had been told we could only take half the books and choosing which to take and which to leave was a sad duty and took days. My books to me were very special friends, most from my student days, and I didn't want to part with any of them. Reading goes all the way back to my beginnings. I sat in my favourite library cum-dining room piling my treasures on the table, remembering with each handful the time and place, event and person connected with each volume. It was like running a film of my life as seen from the library shelf. And this was not to mention Alannah's store.

Mine were all there, from Uncle Eddie Cairney's collection, my father's two shelves from the kitchen cupboard, my own hoard in every house I had, especially in Kellie Lodging, books for all occasions – research, travel, education, religion. Lots of Catholic stuff, of course. In my youth I was, to quote Lord Sachs, former British Chief Rabbi, a 'lapsed Protestant'. I tried to resist my inherited Catholicity but it went deeper than I did. I still float in it today, but am trying to keep my head above water. I may have been influenced in the is timid apostasy by my parent's doctor Beryl Cutler, a Jewish scholar of formidable intellect whose professional visits to his patient at home, my father, often became a discussion and debate of the highest order. Especially when they were joined by our local newsagent who was a Communist diehard but who personally brought in Dad's *Glasgow Herald*. The three of them were a library in themselves and would speak easily of Kierkegaard, Camus, Joyce or Marx, or whoever came up in the conversation. I listened at the table, enthralled. These men were reader all their lives and it showed. They would have been appalled at the break-up of the Cairneys' 3,000-volume library in Auckland.

To them, reading was everything, but most of all, it meant information, learning, recreation, sheer pleasure and escape. Like my father and uncles, I was reading all the way from primary school class to Auckland University, and every book to me was always, and still is, a holiday. When the van from the bookshop came to take away half my store of words, I felt exactly as Alannah must have done when one of her best friends came to collect Calliope, our cat, who was off to find a new home on a farm.

Removal is a wrench. It is like a divorce, so just as I did when I was wrenched from Sheila almost 30 years before, I lost myself in work. Or at least, I intended to, but this time in a rare combination of event and cause, everything I was to do that summer, either due to lack of follow-up, or misunderstanding, or cross purposes, fell through. It was almost as if it were meant to be for I was left with plenty of time to house hunt. I found one, but, when Alannah finally arrived in Glasgow two days before our 28th wedding anniversary, she came, she saw – and hated.

Then, on a rainy evening, a miracle! On our way to yet another address, we passed through the Queen's Park area, which reminds me somewhat of Paris with its tree-lined streets and elegant façades.

'I could live here,' said Alannah from the passenger seat.

Then we saw the property we were looking for – it was a converted church! The flat for sale consisted of the adapted vestry and baptistery and when Alannah first saw the interior with two real church pillars in the sitting room, her jaw dropped, and all she said was, 'WOW!' That was on the Friday night and by the Monday afternoon she was the owner. I am her happy co-tenant and as glad to say that it was within these venerable walls every passing word of this book was written.

I feel I have been a guest at my own life's party. In these pages, I have tried to be honest and make my gratitude clear. My only hope is that there is a glimmer of something, no matter how badly expressed, that will please, amuse or do some good to somebody, encourage them to rethink their own lives in terms of the bigger picture instead of the holiday snap we keep of ourselves in the secret recesses of our ego, hoping nobody will see.

I have spent most of my working life in the public view and from that same public, I have learned more than I ever did at school, college or university. I have been sustained by audiences for more than six decades and I am grateful for their trust. If I had the privilege of showing them their selves in costume, as it were, in the end they made me see myself as a servant of the little good and not just the selfish seeker after fame and fortune. I never became a big star, but I was a working professional actor for a very long time and, if I were able, on occasion, to give someone a lump in the throat or enjoy a tear or two, make them smile or laugh, or cause them to take an in-breath and hold it in the hush, then mine was a job well done. These are not great events, admittedly, but they are all part of the theatre experience, which is there in the end to give people time to feel and *think*. Any art works, in that it adds in some way to the sum of content, and that is no mean feat. It is something I would gladly do again – and again and again. I shall be will be very sorry when that stage door finally closes on me.

'I hope to die well,' she said.

'I hope to die unwell,' said he.

We are all human creatures, therefore, it is logical to assume that origically we were created, that is, made by a creator, whom some of us call God. He has imposed a curfew on us that we call death. All of life is merely the rehearsal for this inevitability. I am no more ready for death than the next man, but once it happens, I know what I should like to happen to that waste product that my body would then be.

I should like to see it checked by an appropriate medical officer from the National Funeral Service to confirm that I have really gone. After which my corpse should be wrapped naked in a practical material that would allow it to be transferred immediately in a van to a morgue and dissected in the interest of medical science and the remains cremated to dust and disposed of in an equally practical manner. It may be divided into four little jars, with one being scattered from the flagstaff in Queen's Park, Glasgow (perhaps leaving a handful to throw on to Celtic Park?). The next should be thrown from the top of The Mound in Edinburgh, the third, into the Thames at Boulter's Lock, Maidenhead, and the last from the slopes of Mount Eden in Auckland, New Zealand. These are the places that have mattered to me in my life for personal and cultural reasons, and I should be glad that my dust should settle there. If this is not possible, then let it all go to the nearest landfill, where it should join all the other dusty rubbish and, by means of carbon dioxide and methane gas, thus eventually go some way to lighting up a whole city. In my sincere opinion, dead bodies are merely waste, and it has been found that waste is a huge potential resource.

What I don't want is any truck with undertakers, those quasi-Victorians with the practiced funeral faces, their obscene luxury cars of liner length, and the forest of expensive flowers. The whole show is outdated and reeks of unseemly profit. Certainly, let them do their jobs as good professionals but let them do so as part of a National Funeral Service and be paid accordingly. Anything to prevent having people worry for the latter part of their lives about how their offspring are going to pay for their funeral. Which is why they load themselves with crippling insurance policies. Nobody should have to pay to die. We should go out as we come in, by courtesy of the country we were born in.

By all means, let there be the memorial service in whichever rite chosen, but with a large photograph of the deceased, and not a coffin, which to all intents and purposes, is empty. How pitiful to dress a remnant in uniform or expensive dress when the person, in soul and spirit, has gone to where all ex-bodies go. Let there be memorial masses, prayers, stories, kind remembrances, not for an empty box on supports, but for the memory of the loved one gone. He or she still exists as long as the memory of them lives.

Similarly, graveyards are old-fashioned. They ought to be converted into pleasing Gardens of Remembrance available to all. There is no need at all for names on monuments of stone that are only allowed to decay. Let these names be in our hearts and in our love for the departed. Let them be remembered at least in their own generation. However loved, time inevitably eases the pain and allows the grieving to fully resume their lives.

Love is the word that must inform death, as it does life. Everything done in its name is worthy and is best felt in silence, which is the only commentary needed. Such a love is in the heart of all of us, deep down and too often unused. The kind of love that sustains prisoners in death camps, sailors lost at sea, climbers on mountain peaks, travellers in jungles, lonely people in high flats, beggars on the streets. This is the common chord great poets have touched on. The feeling which real love engenders is not cloying or sentimental, it is a sturdy intimation of life, a late energy that is there to be used by all in our living – and in our dying.

But whatever happens, I shall follow my old father's example and look forward to the great adventure. Until then I shall persevere in my trio of disciplines: writing, painting and speaking in public for a fee, happy labours that have kept me alive for so long and still living. My only regret is that this sense of fulfilment and ease in work has come to me so late in life, but my delight is that it has come at all. My diary is still open for all offers! Indeed, I hope that on my 100th birthday I will have just finished a painting, have been booked for another lecture tour and be checking the contract for my next book. My only real complaint is that there still aren't enough hours in the day.

As one anonymous writer put it:

Yesterday's act is the deed of today.

Each is writ in tomorrow's blood,

and can never be washed away.

How often have we heard it said of a baby or very young child, 'S/he's been here before'? There may be something in that. It may be eccentric theology, and improbable science, but I like to think that when the body part of me dies and becomes waste, the spirit element or soul, or whatever it is termed, might be recycled, as it were, and used to be fitted to a new child born at the exactly the moment when I died. It seems more practical than having every single human starting entirely from scratch. Better to use energy when it has been proved in a life that has been fully lived. This might not be feasible, of course, but I like to think I might be returned as a black man, an Eskimo or even a member of the royal family.

Whatever the wild theories, life does go on – and on – ending only to begin again like the quasars, the black holes, the meteors, asteroids, planets and stars that continue their dance above us in dark skies that stretch all the way back to eternity and forward into our shared past. Always dying yet always coming alive, continually contradicting yet giving poor humans hope that we too are part of the great wheel that keeps turning. Carrying us on to wherever we are supposed to be going – in this world, or in however many worlds there are. Always hoping to find a new purity of existence – or is it rather an ancient simplicity regained?

In December 1897, Paul Gauguin painted a large canvas entitled 'Where do we come from? What are we? Where are we going to?' in his straw hut in Tahiti. He was ill, depressed and penniless and was contemplating suicide, but he wanted to do at least one big work before he went, so he painted this canvas. He had lost a loved daughter and no longer believed in God. He only knew despair, yet he had the energy to create a masterpiece. How did he do it? Because he hadn't lost his spirit and the spirit is the nearest relation to the soul that we have. And while we have soul we should have hope and while we have hope we have a chance.

I have had a whole lifetime to find out I don't know the answers to Gauguin's questions. There is so much I don't know. All I do know is that I can wait to find out. That will be part of my final adventure. Meantime, we have to respect time because we never know how much of it has been allotted to us. I know I must yield to my body or listen to what my spirit is trying to tell me. Meantime I can only take reassurance from Oscar Wilde, who postulated in his inimitable way, 'If one tells the truth, one is sure, sooner or later, to be found out.' Or again, as Charlie Chaplin said, 'In close-up, life's a tragedy, but in long shot it's a comedy. The only thing to do, therefore, is to try and have the last laugh.'

And, at the same time, we must bear in mind, the medieval couplet:
Keep well the Ten Commandments and flee Sin's deadly Seven,
Spend well the body's senses and you will come to heaven.

I remain faithfully Catholic, although I can't honestly say I approve of much of modern Catholicism. I mourn the loss of the Latin Mass and the old familiar hymns, I resent queuing up for Holy Communion as if at Passport Control, and I am saddened by the overall dumbing down of the basic liturgy and the generally poor standard of the sermons. Although there are exceptions, and one takes in the pearls that occasionally. Only this very morning, Monsignor Murrey said at St Helen's, Langside: 'The whole Bible can be summed up in one sentence from St John – "Almighty God so loved the world that he sent His own Son to die for us so that all shall be saved and none be lost."'

I loved that thought – that none shall be lost. That's what gives me hope. I am glad that the real Catholic voice, such as the Monsignor's, is still to be heard above the general hubbub.

I am not ashamed of having rediscovered the truth surviving at the heart of my religion and I am grateful for the peace and comfort that fact now gives me. It is still the church of my fathers. It always has been and no matter the modern changes, the drop in attendances, its continuing diplomatic errors, the gossip and the scandals, it *is* as it always has been and always will be. *Deo Gratias*.

I was 84 years of age at 4.30 pm on Sunday 16 February 2014. This means I've trodden my life path for more than 30,000 days. That's a lot of rising up and sitting down, eating, sleeping and breathing, but it leaves me with the thought that I have trodden down many of the weeds that had grown under my feet and at last I can begin to see the flowers by the wayside that I missed in my hurry to move onwards and up.

We are not the journey, we are the carriers of ourselves on the way, guardians of our inner workings, a combination of the mechanistic and the human that makes us mortal. It is there right at the core of our being. It has no title, no name, no status, no nationality; it is nothing but the sameness we all share at root and that is what we have to remember if we are to realise the true importance of being.

Endpiece

The end is nigh,
Which is why
I try
Not to think of it.
But drink of it,
This cup of life, which shows
What everyone knows.
That the water of life
Springs from a source,
Of course,
That goes deep.
So why weep about dying,
Stop sighing
And reach for the light.
The white,
Your right,
Your reward for living
For giving
Of your best
In the test
You have passed
At last.
Now you are free
And can really see
What it means
To be.

Acknowledgements

I could count on the fingers of my hand all that is needed for the good life – first is family, next are friends. Friends are fingers. You can't have more than ten – really close friends, I mean. Even then, five is more likely. Acquaintances abound, colleagues are plentiful, but true friends are rare. As the rhyme says:

Some friends are new friends,
Some friends are old.
New friends are silver,
Old friends are gold.
Friendship's like fruit
Especially when
It's tasted by all friends
Again and again.

So be it.

Everyone has their own register, names in their lives, that tell their personal story. This is mine. These are the people met for a moment or known for a lifetime, but all still remembered.

Grandparents John Cairney and Ellen McLaughlin, John Coyle and Agnes O'Neil. Parents Thomas Cairney and Mary Coyle. Brother Jim and sister Agnes. Uncles Eddie and Phil Cairney, Hugh and James Coyle, Aunts Sarah McIlhatton and Grace McNamee. Cousins John Cairney, Margaret Swan, Elizabeth Donaldson, James McNamee, Margaret McNamee, Agnes McCarthy, Philip Cairney, Theresa McIlhatton and Virginia Arbadji. Priests and Fathers Power, Bassett, Tomasi and Ward. Canon Rooney, Monsignor Murray, Bishop Conte, Cardinals Winning and O'Brien. Sister Genaro. Schoolteachers Susan Callaghan and Susan Battye. Doctors Beryl Cutler, Bill Sircus, John Molloy and John Crorie. Street friends Tom Gibson, Tom Gray, Victor Travisari, Felix McKenna, Chic Coia, Bill Preston, Bill Hutcheson, John Donnelly, Bill Preston and Tony Kempton. School friends Bobby Gibson, Dr Gerald McGrath, John Kirk, John Davitt, Jackie Devlin, Frank McGuire and Peter McCafferty. College friends Andy Stewart, Jimmy Copeland, John Grieve, David McKail, Sheila Newbigging and Ellen McIntosh. University friends Ian Laing and Dr Kirsten

McCue. Drama lecturers Colin Chandler, Geoffrey Nethercott, Marie Pirie and John Arnott. Professors Ian Gordon, David Daichies, Bill Murray, Gerard Carruthers and David Purdie. Academics Dr Marshall Walker, Dr Mike Paterson and Dr Monica Barry. Theatre colleagues John Fraser, Roddy McMillan, Duncan Macrae, Andrew Keir, Fulton Mackay, Rikki Fulton, Ronald Hines, Peter O'Toole, Leonard Maguire, Tony Roper, Tom Fleming, Patrick Troughton, Liz Maclennan, David Maclennan, Juliet Cadzow, David McKail, Bruce Mason and John Callan. Television colleagues Robert Urquhart, Frank Finlay, Nigel Green, Donald Douglas, Alistair Sim, John Laurie, and Dame Maggie Smith. Film colleagues Dirk Bogarde, Peter Finch, John Gregson, Kenneth More, David McCallum, Bill Simpson, Alan Cumming, Brian Cox, Ian Bannen, Donal Donnelly, Richard Harris, James Cagney, Sir Michael Redgrave, Richard Burton, Michael Williams, Simon Callow, John Sessions, Jeanne Craine, Dames Judi Dench and Elizabeth Taylor. Theatre Directors Tony Guthrie, Callum Mill, John Moody, Gerard Slevin Dr Donald Smith, Stephen Callaghan, and Sir Richard Eyre. Television Directors Pharic McLaren, James Mac-Taggart and Ian McNaughten. Film directors Michael Powell, Ronald Neame, Michael Anderson, John Boulting and Robin Crichton. Singers Moira Anderson, Jean Redpath, Maria Callas, Isobel Buchanan, Ann Hetherington, Alicia Devine, Kenneth McKellar, Callum Kennedy, Alastair McDonald and Sammy San. Comedians Jimmy Logan, Billy Connolly and Andy Cameron. Composers Geoff Davidson and Gordon Rigby. Poets Angus Reid, Matt McGinn, Hugh MacDiarmid, Iain Crawford, Pam Ayres, Kirsty Cleary and Rab Wilson. Playwrights Arthur Miller. John McGrath, Tom Wright, John Arden and Bill Bryden. Scriptwriters Jack Gerson, Karen Curtis and Gerry McDade. Writers Alanna Knight, William McIlvanney, Cecil P Taylor, James Murray, Timothy Neat, John Cargill Thomson, Dr Donald Smith, Jim Wilkie, Dan Cleary. Artists Ian Fleming, John Byrne, Anneke Laan, Louise Annand, Gordon Cockburn, Philip Raskin, Joyce Gunn Cairns, George Devlin, Peter Howsen and Sir Stanley Spencer. Curators Elspeth King, Michael Donnelly, Liz Kwaznick, Nat Edwards and Natsha Raskin. Film animator Ray Harryhaussen, Cartoonist Jack Stokes, Sculptor Benno Schotz. Iconist Jenny Trolove. Architects John Coleman and John Thomson. Radio Producer James Crampsey and John O'Leary. Record Producers Norman Newall and Neil Ross. Librarians Lesley Johnson and Dr Alan Marchbanks. Publishers John Calder, Bob Ross, Helen Benton, Bill Campbell, Peter MacKenzie and

ACKNOWLEDGEMENTS

Gavin MacDougall. Editors Judith Sleigh, Alan Bruce, Jennie Renton, Harriet Allan, Lydia Novak and Louise Hutcheson. Journalists Clare Brotherwood, Alan Taylor, John Gibson, Jimmy Reid, Jack Webster and Amanda Dickie. Lawyers James Farrell. Stuart Jeffrey, Leonard Murray, Tim Cleary, Sean Baldwin and Judge Kitty Forrest. Agents Christopher Mann, John Caddell, Barry Krost and Ann Thomas. Manager Colin Harvey Wright and Wallace Overton. Secretaries Jennifer and Valerie Castle, Susan Frame. Promoters Jim Haynes, John Worth, John McQuaig, Robert Keedick, Emmet Hobbs and Craig Sim. Banker Graham Buchanan, Accountants Bob Adams and Alan Carmichael. Politician Jean Urquhart. Civil Servant Ernest Meyhew. Researchers Pat Woods and Tom Campbell. Footballers Jim Craig and Billy McNeill. Boxer Muhammad Ali. Hotelier Hugh Grant, Restaurateur Tony Matteo. Publican Margaret and Matthew Reilly. Company Director David Clarkson and Entrepreneurs Alex Farquar and David Lambert. Naturopath Claire Newall-Simpson. Hairdresser Tommy Fleming, Jeweller Marshall Caldwell. Publicist John Morgan. Burnsians Dr Jim McKay, Jock Thomson, Jim Sheilds and Murdo Morrison. The Earl and Countess of Elgin. Neighbours Kay Caldwell and Joe McGinley, James and Eileen Collins, Ioan and Samantha Jones. Then there are the original minds: William Cowan, Janie Dawson, Kay O'Leary, Starley Thompson, Ray Neale, Robin Hyde, Michael Stopforth, Pat Baldwin, Paddy Cleary. Bill Livingstone, Kath Hill and Eleanor Manners Female influences Mary Theresa McFarlane, Margaret Swan, Nell Brennan, Maureen Braid, Philippa Reid, Virginia Green and Mary Corboy. Sisters-in-law Colleen Cleary, Aileen O'Sullivan, Patsy Baldwin, Miki Neale and Josie Trolove. My Godchildren Branwell Johnson, Sarah Duckworth and Jacinta Kalsey. My first wife, Sheila Parker Cowan. Our children, Jennifer Cairney, Alison Hill, Lesley Manners, Jane Livingstone and Jonathan Cairney. My sons-in-law, Derek Hill, Stewart Manners and Iain Livingstone. Their children, my grandchildren, Liam, Scarlett and Ivy Hill, Georgia, Freya and Liberty Manners, Sylvie, Louisa and Hope Livingstone. How good it is to have HOPE at the end of the line.

But the first and last name must be that of my wife, best pal, indispensible colleague, business partner, first critic and daily inspiration:
ALANNAH MARY O'SULLIVAN.
She is all to me.

185

And now, if only to complete the record, I am, at the time of writing:

Male, Aquarian, Scottish-born, UK national, Glaswegian, Roman
Catholic, Celtic Supporter, Marist schoolboy, Altar boy, Choir boy,
Office boy, Art student, RAF National Serviceman, Drama student,
Actor, Singer, Director, Producer, Company Director, Author, Lyricist,
Songwriter, Lecturer, Designer, Painter, Raconteur, Husband, Father,
Grandfather, Godfather, New Zealand national, Socialist, Pacifist,
Diploma in Dramatic Studies, Bachelor of Arts, Master of Literature,
Doctor of Philosophy, Member of the Incorporation of Bonnet-
Makers and Dyers of Glasgow, Artist Member of the Glasgow Art
Club, Life Member of British Actors' Equity, Honorary Rotarian,
Honorary Member of the Falkirk Burns Club, Honorary President of
the Robert Burns Guild of Speakers, Honorary President of the
Robert Burns World Federation, Honorary Citizen of Winnipeg,
Manitoba, a Freeman Citizen of Glasgow and an Archive in the
Special Theatre Collections at the University of Glasgow.

Greasepaint Monkey:
An Actor on Acting

John Cairney

ISBN: 978-1-906817-42-8 PBK £10.99

A book for actors, for would-be actors and for everyone who has a curiosity about theatre as it is on the inside. Legendary actor, John Cairney, explores what actors have been doing off and on stage as they go about their business of pretending to be someone else in public for money.

As someone who has spent his professional lifetime acting, he lifts the mask he wears, looks backstage and invites the audience right into the rehearsal room. He puts the spotlight on the mystery behind the mystique, the sweat beneath the greasepaint and the excitement to be found in the second oldest trade in the world.

Glasgow By the Way, But

John Cairney

ISBN: 978-1-906307-10-3 PBK £7.99

Glasgow to me is the ugly face that launched a thousand quips. If you're born in Glasgow you're born with a sense of humour. It's the only passport you need to get beyond its boundaries.

In this collection of personal anecdotes, John Cairney takes you on a tour of *his* Glasgow, introducing the people and places that have shaped it. Full of the humour, tension and patter that characterises Scotland's most charismatic city, everyone will be sure to find a part of their own Glasgow reflected in Cairney's honest evocation of his home city.

The Quest for Charles Rennie Mackintosh

John Cairney

ISBN: 978-1-905222-43-8 PBK £8.99

For the last 30 years John Cairney has been on a personal quest to find the complex man behind the façade that was Charles Rennie Mackintosh, architect and artist. Though recognised even in his own day as a genius, he was by no means a pre-Raphaelite plaster-cast saint of high morals and mystic vision. He was a flesh and blood charmer, who attracted women as much as he irritated men, enjoyed a drink to a sometimes excessive degree and was known for his explosive temper and black moods. He was all artist, but also all man, with the advantages and disadvantages of both.

The Quest for Robert Louis Stevenson

John Cairney

ISBN: 978 1842820 85 0 PBK £8.99

John Cairney offers an original perspective on Scotland's finest writer of English prose, examining the intimate relationships in the life of Robert Louis Stevenson. A puzzle to his friends and family in his lifetime, Stevenson still remains something of an enigma, even to enthusiasts. Years of restless wandering led him to tropical Samoa, where he found not only well-being, but a release of the passionate potential that had been in him from his chilly beginnings in Edinburgh. This virtual paradise, however, was marred by the eccentric behaviour of his wife. In this book, John Cairney explores their relationship and other fascinating aspects of Stevenson's life.

On The Trail of Robert Burns

John Cairney

ISBN: 978-0-946487-51-6 PBK £7.99

Is there anything new to say about Robert Burns? John Cairney says it's time to trash Burns the Brand and come on the trail of the real Robert Burns. He is the best of travelling companions on this entertaining journey to the heart of the Burns story. Internationally known as 'the face of Robert Burns', John Cairney believes that the traditional Burns tourist trail urgently needs to find a new direction. In an acting career spanning 40 years he has often lived and breathed Robert burns on stage. *On the Trail of Robert Burns* shows just how well he has got under the skin of Burn's complex character. This fascinating journey around Scotland is a rediscovery of Scotland's national bard as a flesh and blood genius.

The Luath Burns Companion

John Cairney

ISBN: 978 1906817 85 5 PBK £9.99

This is not another 'complete works' but a personal selection from 'The Man Who Played Robert Burns' – John Cairney. His favourites are reproduced here and he talks about them with an obvious love of the man and his work. His depth of knowledge and understanding has been garnered over 40 years of study, writing and performance.

Burns' work has drama, passion, pathos and humour. His careful workmanship is concealed by the spontaneity of his verse. He was always a forward thinking man and remains a writer for the future.

Immortal Memories: A Compilation of Toasts to Robert Burns

John Cairney

ISBN: 978 1905222 48 3 PBK £12.99

The annual Burns Supper, a cult in virtually every country in the world, is an occasion when people gather around a dinner table to give tribute to a Scottish poet who died more than 200 years ago. It really is an extraordinary phenomenon.
JOHN CAIRNEY

To be asked to deliver the 'Immortal Memory' – the chief toast and center-piece of the traditional Burns Supper – is recognised as a privilege by Burns enthusiasts the world over. *Immortal Memories* is an extensive collection of these toasts from around the world (together with other orations, verses and addresses), spanning the two hundred years from the first Burns Supper in Alloway in 1801.

Burnscripts: Dramatic Interpretations of the Life and Art of Robert Burns

John Cairney

ISBN: 978-1-906817-72-5 PBK £14.99

Burnscripts is a collection of dramatic scripts by John Cairney interpreting the life and works of Robert Burns.

Cairney, as actor, author and scriptwriter, has been connected professionally with Robert Burns for nearly half a century. He has performed as Burns all over the world and consequently knows him better than most.

This personal exploration of Burns' life and work in performance helps to build a fuller picture of the poet and is an insightful celebration of one of Scotland's most important cultural icons.

Details of these and other books published by Luath Press can be found at:
www.luath.co.uk

Luath Press Limited
committed to publishing well written books worth reading

LUATH PRESS takes its name from Robert Burns, whose little collie Luath (*Gael.*, swift or nimble) tripped up Jean Armour at a wedding and gave him the chance to speak to the woman who was to be his wife and the abiding love of his life.
Burns called one of 'The Twa Dogs' Luath after Cuchullin's hunting dog in Ossian's *Fingal*. Luath Press was established in 1981 in the heart of Burns country, and now resides a few steps up the road from Burns' first lodgings on Edinburgh's Royal Mile.
Luath offers you distinctive writing with a hint of unexpected pleasures.

Most bookshops in the UK, the US, Canada, Australia, New Zealand and parts of Europe either carry our books in stock or can order them for you. To order direct from us, please send a £sterling cheque, postal order, international money order or your credit card details (number, address of cardholder and expiry date) to us at the address below. Please add post and packing as follows: UK – £1.00 per delivery address; overseas surface mail – £2.50 per delivery address; overseas airmail – £3.50 for the first book to each delivery address, plus £1.00 for each additional book by airmail to the same address. If your order is a gift, we will happily enclose your card or message at no extra charge.

ILLUSTRATION: IAN KELLAS

Luath Press Limited
543/2 Castlehill
The Royal Mile
Edinburgh EH1 2ND
Scotland

Telephone: 0131 225 4326 (24 hours)
email: sales@luath.co.uk
Website: www.luath.co.uk